THE BOOK OF SECRETS

Healing the Heart

Everyday Immortality

The Lords of the Light

On the Shores of Eternity

How to Know God

The Soul in Love

The Chopra Center Herbal Handbook
(with coauthor David Simon)

Grow Younger, Live Longer
(with coauthor David Simon)

The Deeper Wound

The Chopra Center Cookbook
(coauthored by David Simon and Leanne Backer)

The Angel Is Near

The Daughters of Joy

Golf for Enlightenment

Soulmate

The Spontaneous Fulfillment of Desire

Peace Is the Way

Magical Beginnings, Enchanted Lives
(with David Simon, M.D., and Vicki Abrams, C.C.E., I.B.C.L.C.)

DEEPAK CHOPRA, M.D.

The BOOK *of* SECRETS

*Unlocking
the Hidden Dimensions
of Your Life*

THREE RIVERS PRESS • NEW YORK

Three Rivers Press and the Tugboat design are registered trademarks
of Random House, Inc.

Originally published in hardcover in the United States by
Harmony Books, an imprint of the Crown Publishing Group,
a division of Random House, Inc., New York, in 2004.

Library of Congress Cataloging-in-Publication Data
Chopra, Deepak.
The book of secrets : unlocking the hidden
dimensions of your life / Deepak Chopra.
1. Spiritual life.   2. Meditations.   3. Life skills.   I. Title.
BL624.C4764 2004
158.1—dc22   2004011311

ISBN 1-4000-9834-3

Printed in the United States of America

Design by Lynne Amft

24 26 28 30 29 27 25 23

First Paperback Edition

To my father,

KRISHAN LAL CHOPRA:

your graceful life and your graceful death

inspired and finally unlocked

the hidden dimensions of my life.

ACKNOWLEDGMENTS

Peter Guzzardi, my very skillful editor:
you are both my critic and one of my best friends;

Shaye, Tina, Tara, Brian, Jenny,
and the rest of my family at Harmony:
you have been loving, gracious, and tolerant
since the beginning of my career;

Rita, Mallika, Gotham, Sumant, Candice, and darling Tara:
you make everything worthwhile and sacred;

Carolyn Rangel, Felicia Rangel, and Jan Crawford in my office:
your dedication and hard work make everything possible;

And finally, thanks to my family at the Chopra Center,
who translate my words into a practice
that makes a difference in people's lives.

CONTENTS

CONTENTS

THE BOOK OF SECRETS

OPENING THE BOOK
OF SECRETS

THE GREATEST HUNGER in life is not for food, money, success, status, security, sex, or even love from the opposite sex. Time and again people have achieved all of these things and wound up still feeling dissatisfied—indeed, often more dissatisfied than when they began. The deepest hunger in life is a secret that is revealed only when a person is willing to unlock a hidden part of the self. In the ancient traditions of wisdom, this quest has been likened to diving for the most precious pearl in existence, a poetic way of saying that you have to swim far out beyond shallow waters, plunge deep into yourself, and search patiently until the pearl beyond price is found.

The pearl is also called essence, the breath of God, the water of life, holy nectar—labels for what we, in our more prosaic scientific age, would simply call transformation. Transformation means radical change of form, the way a caterpillar transforms into a butterfly. In human terms, it means turning fear, aggression, doubt, insecurity, hatred, and emptiness into their opposites. Can this really be achieved? One thing we know for certain: The secret hunger that gnaws at people's souls has nothing to do with externals like money, status, and security. It's the inner person who craves meaning in life, the end of suffering, and answers to the riddles of love, death, God, the soul, good and evil. A life spent on the surface will never answer these questions or satisfy the needs that drive us to ask them.

Finding the hidden dimensions in yourself is the only way to fulfill your deepest hunger.

After the rise of science, this craving for knowledge should have faded, but it has only grown stronger. There are no new "facts" to discover about life's hidden dimensions. Nobody needs to peer at more CAT scans of patients undergoing a near-death experience or take more MRIs of yogis sitting deep in meditation. That phase of experimentation has done its work: We can be assured that wherever consciousness wants to go, the human brain will follow. Our neurons are capable of registering the highest spiritual experiences. In some ways, however, you and I know less about the mystery of life than our ancestors.

We live in the Age of the Higher Brain, the cerebral cortex that has grown enormously over the last few millennia, overshadowing the ancient, instinctive lower brain. The cortex is often called the new brain, yet the old brain held sway in humans for millions of years, as it does today in most living things. The old brain can't conjure up ideas or read. But it does possess the power to feel and, above all, to be. It was the old brain that caused our forebears to sense the closeness of a mysterious presence everywhere in Nature.

That presence, which is found in every particle of creation, suffuses your life, too. You are a book of secrets waiting to be opened, although you probably see yourself in totally different terms. On a given day, you are a worker, a father or mother, husband or wife, a consumer combing the mall stores for something new, an audience member waiting impatiently for the next entertainment.

When you are living the truth of one reality, every secret reveals itself without effort or struggle.

It comes down to the age-old choice of separation or unity. Do you want to be fragmented, conflicted, torn between the eternal forces of darkness and light? Or do you want to step out of separation into wholeness? You are a creature who acts, thinks, and feels. Spirituality fuses these three into a single reality. Thinking doesn't lord it over feeling; feeling doesn't stubbornly resist the higher brain; doing occurs when both thought and feeling say, "This is right." The one reality can be recognized because once you are there, you experience the flow of life without obstacles or resistance. In this flow, you encounter inspiration, love, truth, beauty, and wisdom as natural aspects of existence. The one reality is spirit, and the surface of life is only a disguise with a thousand masks that keeps us from discovering what is real. A thousand years ago, such a statement would have met with no argument. Spirit was accepted everywhere as the true source of life. Today, we have to look with new eyes at the mystery of existence, for as proud children of science and reason, we have made ourselves the orphans of wisdom.

Therefore, this book must work on two fronts. First, it must persuade you that there really is a mystery lying in the hidden dimensions of life. Second, it must inspire you to feel the passion and dedication required to get there. This isn't a project to postpone until you are ready. You have been ready since the day you forgot to keep asking who you are and why you are here. Sadly, most of us keep shutting out thousands of experiences that could make transformation a reality. If it weren't for the enormous effort we put into denial, repression, and doubt, each life would be a constant revelation.

Ultimately you have to believe that your life is worth investigating with total passion and commitment. It took thousands of tiny decisions to keep the book of secrets closed, but it takes only a single moment to open it again.

I take it literally when the New Testament says, "Ask and you will receive, knock and the door will be opened." It's that simple.

You will know every secret about life when you can truly say *I must know. I can't wait a moment longer.* Buddha sitting under the Bodhi tree and Jesus wrestling with demons in the desert are symbolic of the same drama of the soul that you were born to repeat. Never doubt this: You are the most significant being in the world, because at the level of the soul you *are* the world. You don't have to earn the right to know. Your very next thought, feeling, or action can begin to uncover the deepest spiritual wisdom, which flows as pure and free as mountain waters in spring. It isn't possible for the self to keep secrets from itself forever, no matter how thoroughly we've been trained to believe otherwise.

❀

THE MYSTERY
OF LIFE IS REAL

THE LIFE YOU KNOW is a thin layer of events covering a deeper reality. In the deeper reality, you are part of every event that is happening now, has ever happened, or ever will happen. In the deeper reality, you know absolutely who you are and what your purpose is. There is no confusion or conflict with any other person on earth. Your purpose in life is to help creation to expand and grow. When you look at yourself, you see only love.

The mystery of life isn't any of these things, however. It's how to bring them to the surface. If someone asked me how to prove that there really is a mystery of life, the simplest proof would be just this enormous separation between deep reality and everyday existence. Ever since you and I were born, we've had a constant stream of clues hinting at another world inside ourselves. Haven't you ever fallen into a moment of wonder? Such moments may come in the presence of beautiful music, or at the sight of natural beauty that sends a shiver up your spine. Or you may have looked out of the corner of your eye at something familiar—morning sunlight, a tree swaying in the wind, the face of someone you love as he or she sleeps—knowing in that moment that life was more than it appears to be.

Countless clues have come your way, only to be overlooked because they didn't form a clear message. I have met an astonishing number of people whose spiritual beginnings were nothing short of amazing: As children, they may have seen a grandmother's soul leave at the moment of her death, witnessed beings of light surrounding on a birthday, traveled beyond their physical bodies, or come home from school to see a beloved family member standing in the hallway, even though the person had just died in a terrible auto accident. (One man told me he was a "bubble boy" for the first ten years of his life, journeying in his bubble high over the city and away to unknown lands.) Millions of people—this is no exaggeration but testimony from public polls—have seen themselves bathed in a pearlescent white light at times. Or they heard a voice they knew came from God. Or they had invisible guardians in childhood, secret friends who protected them while they slept.

Eventually, it became clear to me that more people have had such experiences—truly secret voyages into a reality separated from this one by a flimsy veil of disbelief—than not. Parting the veil means changing your own perception. This is a personal, totally subjective, yet very real shift.

Where would you begin to solve a mystery that is everywhere, yet somehow never forms a whole message? A great sleuth like Sherlock Holmes would start his search from one elementary deduction: *Something unknown wants to be known.* A mystery that doesn't want to be known will just keep retreating the closer you come to it. The mystery of life doesn't behave that way: Its secrets are revealed immediately if you know where to look. But where is that?

The body's wisdom is a good entry point into the hidden dimensions of life, because although completely invisible, the body's wisdom is undeniably real—a fact that medical researchers began to accept in the mid-1980s. The former view was that the brain's capacity for intelligence was unique. But then signs of intelligence began to be discovered in the immune system, and then in the digestive system. In both these systems, special messenger molecules could be observed circulating through every organ, bringing information to and from the brain, but also functioning on their own. A white cell that can distinguish between invading enemy bacteria and harmless pollen is making an intelligent decision, even though it floats in the bloodstream apart from the brain.

Ten years ago, it would have seemed absurd to speak of intestines being intelligent. The lining of the digestive tract was known to possess thousands of nerve endings, but these were just remote outposts of the nervous system—a way for it to keep in touch with the lowly business of extracting nutrition from food. Now it turns out that the intestines are not so lowly after all. Their scattered nerve cells form a finely tuned system for reacting to outside events—an upsetting remark at work, the threat of danger, a death in the family. The stomach's reactions are just as reliable as the brain's thoughts, and just as intricate. Your colon, your liver, and your stomach cells also *think,* only not in the brain's verbal language. What people had been calling a "gut reaction" turned out to be a mere hint of the complex intelligence at work in a hundred thousand billion cells.

In a sweeping medical revolution, scientists have stepped into a hidden dimension that no one had ever suspected. Cells have been outthinking us for millions of years. In fact, their wisdom, more ancient than cortical wisdom, could be the best model for the only thing more ancient than they, which is the cosmos. Perhaps the universe has been outthinking us, too. No matter where I look, I sense what cosmic wisdom is trying to accomplish. It is much the same as what I myself want to accomplish—to grow, expand, and create— the main difference being that my body is cooperating with the universe better than I manage to.

Cells have no problem fully participating in the mystery of life. Theirs is a wisdom of total passion and commitment. So let's see if we can link the qualities of bodily wisdom with the hidden dimensions we want to uncover:

THE WISDOM YOU ARE
ALREADY LIVING

Identifying with the Body's Intelligence

1. You have a **higher purpose.**
2. You are in **communion** with the whole of life.
3. Your **awareness** is always open to change. From moment to moment, it senses everything in your environment.
4. You feel **acceptance** for all others as your equal, without judgment or prejudice.
5. You seize every moment with renewed **creativity,** not clinging to the old and outworn.
6. Your **being** is cradled in the rhythms of the universe. You feel safe and nurtured.
7. Your idea of **efficiency** is to let the flow of life bring you what you need. Force, control, and struggle are not your way.
8. You feel a sense of **connection** with your source.
9. You are committed to **giving** as the source of all abundance.
10. You see all change, including birth and death, against the background of **immortality.** Whatever is unchanging is most real to you.

None of these items are spiritual aspirations; they are facts of daily existence at the level of your cells.

Higher purpose: Every cell in your body agrees to work for the welfare of the whole; its individual welfare comes second. If necessary, it will die to protect the body, and often does—the lifetime of any given cell is a fraction of our own lifetime. Skin cells perish by the thousands every hour, as do immune cells fighting off invading microbes. Selfishness is not an option, even when it comes to a cell's own survival.

Communion: A cell keeps in touch with every other cell. Messenger molecules race everywhere to notify the body's farthest outposts of desire or intention, however slight. Withdrawing or refusing to communicate is not an option.

Awareness: Cells adapt from moment to moment. They remain flexible in order to respond to immediate situations. Getting caught up in rigid habits is not an option.

Acceptance: Cells recognize each other as equally important. Every function in the body is interdependent with every other. Going it alone is not an option.

Creativity: Although every cell has a set of unique functions (liver cells, for example, can perform fifty separate tasks), these combine in creative ways. A person can digest food never eaten before, think thoughts never thought before, dance in a way never seen before. Clinging to old behavior is not an option.

Being: Cells obey the universal cycle of rest and activity. Although this cycle expresses itself in many ways, such as fluctuating hormone levels, blood pressures, and digestive rhythms, the most obvious expression is sleep. Why we need to sleep remains a medical mystery, yet complete dysfunction develops if we don't enjoy its benefits. In the silence of inactivity, the future of the body is incubating. Being obsessively active or aggressive is not an option.

Efficiency: Cells function with the smallest possible expenditure of energy. Typically, a cell stores only three seconds of food and oxygen inside its cell wall. It trusts totally on being provided for. Excessive consumption of food, air, or water is not an option.

Bonding: Due to their common genetic inheritance, cells know that they are fundamentally the same. The fact that liver cells are different from heart cells, and muscle cells are different from brain cells, does not negate their common identity, which is unchanging. In the laboratory, a muscle cell can be genetically transformed into a heart cell by going back to their common source. Healthy cells remain tied to their source no matter how many times they divide. For them, being an outcast is not an option.

Giving: The primary activity of cells is giving, which maintains the integrity of all other cells. Total commitment to giving makes receiving automatic—it is the other half of a natural cycle. Hoarding is not an option.

Immortality: Cells reproduce in order to pass on their knowledge, experience, and talents, withholding nothing from their offspring. This is a kind of practical immortality, submitting to death on the physical plane but defeating it on the nonphysical. The generation gap is not an option.

When I look at what my cells have agreed to, isn't it a spiritual pact in every sense of the word? The first quality, following a higher purpose, is the same as the spiritual qualities of surrender and selflessness. Giving is the same as returning to God what is God's. Immortality is the same as a belief in life after death. The labels adopted by the mind are not my body's concern, however. To my body, these qualities are simply the way life works. They are the result of cosmic intelligence expressing itself over billions of years as biology. The mystery of life was patient and careful in allowing its full potential to emerge. Even now, the silent agreement that holds my body together feels like a secret because, to all appearances, this agreement doesn't exist. More than two hundred and fifty types of cells go about their daily business: The fifty functions that a liver cell performs are totally unique, not overlapping with the tasks of muscle, kidney, heart, or brain cells—yet it would be catastrophic if even one function were compromised. The mystery of life has found a way to express itself perfectly through me.

Scan the list of qualities again and take note of everything marked "not an option": selfishness, refusing to communicate, living like an outcast, overconsumption, obsessive activity, and aggression. If our cells know not to behave in these ways, why do we? Why is greed good for us and yet spells destruction at the level of our cells, where greed is the basic mistake made by cancer cells? Why do we allow overconsumption to lead to an epidemic of obesity when our cells measure to the molecule how much fuel to consume? The very behavior that would kill our bodies in a day hasn't been renounced by us as people. We are betraying our bodily wisdom, and worse, we are ignoring the model of a perfect spiritual life inside ourselves.

This book was not born out of a sense that people are spiritually weak and inadequate. It was born from a moment of crisis in my family that gave me new hope instead. My father died a few years ago when no one expected it. Still vigorous at eighty-one, he had spent that January day watching a new U.S. president being inaugurated. Retired from his long medical practice as a cardiologist, my father still kept a professional hand in, and he had spent that evening discussing medical cases with a circle of his students.

My mother, who was sleeping in a separate room because of poor health, didn't hear Krishan go to bed. But after midnight, when she was still unable to sleep, he appeared at her door in his bedclothes, barely a dim outline in the darkness, and said that he was leaving. Immediately my mother knew what he meant. My father kissed her goodbye and said that he loved her. Then he padded quietly back to his room where only the night sounds of crickets, tropical birds, and Delhi traffic penetrated. He lay down, called to God three times, and died.

Our family was swept up in turmoil. My younger brother and I rushed to India from the United States as fast as we could, and within hours, having traditionally dressed my father's body for the funeral and strewn it with marigolds, we carried it downstairs to the wailing of women mixed with sacred chanting. Not long after that, I was standing over a pile of ashes at the burning *ghat* by the river, performing the eldest son's duty of smashing the remains of the skull with a stick to symbolically release the earthly bonds to the life my father had led.

I couldn't escape the feeling that he had completely and utterly disappeared, this man who had been the most loved person in my life and the last one I thought of losing so soon. But the fact that he had passed with such clear, calm awareness kept all of us from feeling the deepest pangs of grief. Although I was certain Krishan Chopra was gone in the form of the body and personality I knew, my emotions couldn't rest until I articulated, in every detail possible, what he had become. The mystery was changing him from one state to another, and I realized that the same transformation is happening in myself and in everyone. We are all held together and we all dissolve according to mystery, nothing else.

Instead of investigating the mystery of life as an intimate part of ourselves, we've been acting as if it doesn't exist. Everyone has suffered for this neglect, and more suffering, perhaps on an unheard-of scale, is looming over the horizon. My father departed from a world sunk in the depths of gloom. When the evening news comes on tonight, trouble will be breaking out everywhere, as it always is, and the answers being offered won't be anywhere close to the wisdom of a single cell. Many people lose heart and withdraw from the challenge of so much suffering. Others assume that they must leave where they are and find something they do not yet have—a new relationship, a new job, a new religion or teacher—before they can feel alive again.

Would the cells in your body accept such defeatist logic? If where you are isn't good enough, then love and healing and God will remain forever out of reach. After generations of life spent in chaos, are we ready to let the mystery save us now? Is there any other way?

CHANGING YOUR REALITY TO
ACCOMMODATE THE FIRST SECRET

Each secret will be matched with an exercise to allow you to apply it to yourself. Reading about a secret has an effect at the level of thinking; the level of feeling and the level of doing remain untouched. All three have to merge before you are actually changing your personal reality.

The first secret is to let your body's wisdom point the way. Today, write down the ten qualities of this wisdom mentioned earlier, and for each one, think of a way you could live that quality. Note it down and make this your guide for the day. You can pursue one quality per day or list them all and try to follow as many as you can. Don't strain for self-improvement; don't write from a sense that you are weak or inadequate. The purpose here is to extend your body's comfort zone into behavior and feeling. Let your words express aspirations near your heart that make you feel like your true self. For example:

Higher purpose: I am here to serve. I am here to inspire. I am here to love. I am here to live my truth.

Communion: I will appreciate someone who doesn't know that I feel that way. I will overlook the tension and be friendly to someone who has ignored me. I will express at least one feeling that has made me feel guilty or embarrassed.

Awareness: I will spend ten minutes observing instead of speaking. I will sit quietly by myself just to sense how my body feels. If someone irritates me, I will ask myself what I really feel beneath the anger—and I won't stop paying attention until the anger is gone.

Acceptance: I will spend five minutes thinking about the best qualities of someone I really dislike. I will read about a group that I consider totally intolerant and try to see the world as they do. I will look in the mirror and describe myself exactly as if I were the perfect mother or father I wish I had had (beginning with the sentence "How beautiful you are in my eyes").

Creativity: I will imagine five things I could do that my family would never expect—and then I will do at least one of them. I will outline a novel based on my life (every incident will be true, but no one would ever guess that I am the hero). I will invent something in my mind that the world desperately needs.

Being: I will spend half an hour in a peaceful place doing nothing except feeling what it is like to exist. I will lie outstretched on the grass and feel the earth languidly revolving under me. I will take in three breaths and let them out as gently as possible.

Efficiency: I will let at least two things out of my control and see what happens. I will gaze at a rose and reflect on whether I could make it open faster or more beautifully than it already does—then I will ask if my life has blossomed this efficiently. I will lie in a quiet place by the ocean, or with a tape of the sea, and breathe in its rhythms.

Bonding: When I catch myself looking away from someone, I will remember to look into the person's eyes. I will bestow a loving gaze on someone I have taken for granted. I will express sympathy to someone who needs it, preferably a stranger.

Giving: I will buy lunch and give it to someone in need on the street (or I will go to a café and eat lunch with the person). I will compliment someone for a quality that I know the individual values in him- or herself. I will give my children as much of my undivided time today as they want.

Immortality: I will read a scripture about the soul and the promise of life after death. I will write down five things I want my life to be remembered for. I will sit and silently experience the gap between breathing in and breathing out, feeling the eternal in the present moment.

Exercise #2: Accident or Intelligence?

Every secret in this book goes back to the existence of an invisible intelligence that operates beneath the visible surface of life. The mystery of life is an expression not of random accidents but of one intelligence that exists everywhere. Is such an intelligence believable, or should you continue to believe in random events and chance causation?

Read the following unexplained facts; then check *Yes* or *No* if you already knew that such mysteries exist.

Yes ❑ No ❑ Desert birds living by the Grand Canyon bury thousands of pine nuts in widely scattered locations along the canyon rim. They retrieve this stored food during the winter, returning precisely to the nuts each one buried and finding them under a deep layer of snow.

Yes ❑ No ❑ Salmon born in a small stream that feeds the Columbia River in the Pacific Northwest swim out to sea. After several years spent roaming vast distances of ocean, they return to spawn at the precise place where they were born, never winding up in the wrong stream.

Yes ❑ No ❑ Little children from several countries were read to in Japanese; afterward they were asked to pick whether they had just heard some nonsense words or a lovely Japanese poem. The children from Japan all got the answer right, but so did significantly more than half the children from other countries who had never listened to a word of Japanese in their lives.

Yes ❑ No ❑ Identical twins hundreds or thousands of miles apart have immediately sensed the moment when their sibling died in an accident.

Yes ❏ No ❏ Fireflies in Indonesia numbering in the millions are able to synchronize their flashes over an area of several square miles.

Yes ❏ No ❏ In Africa, certain trees that are being overforaged can signal other trees miles away to increase the tannin in their leaves, a chemical that makes them inedible to foraging animals. The distant trees receive the message and alter their chemistry accordingly.

Yes ❏ No ❏ Twins separated at birth have met for the first time years later, only to find that they've each married a woman with the same first name in the same year and now have the same number of children.

Yes ❏ No ❏ Mother albatrosses returning to a nesting site with food in their beaks immediately locate their chicks among hundreds of thousands of identical offspring on a crowded beach.

Yes ❏ No ❏ Once a year at the full moon several million horse-shoe crabs emerge together on one beach to mate. They have answered the same call, from depths of the ocean where no light ever penetrates.

Yes ❏ No ❏ When air molecules cause your eardrum to quiver no differently from a cymbal being hit with a stick, you hear a voice that you recognize speaking words you understand.

Yes ❏ No ❏ On their own, sodium and chlorine are deadly poisons. When they combine as salt, they form the most basic chemical in support of life.

Yes ❏ No ❏ To read this sentence, several million neurons in your cerebral cortex had to form an instantaneous pattern that is completely original and never appeared before in your life.

There is no grade for this exercise, but keep it at hand until you finish this book. Then return to see if your beliefs have changed enough that you can give an explanation based on the spiritual secrets being discussed.

THE WORLD IS IN YOU

TO SOLVE THE MYSTERY OF LIFE requires only one commandment: *Live like a cell.* But we don't, and the reason is not hard to find. We have our own way of doing things. Our cells are fueled by the same oxygen and glucose that fueled amoebas two billion years ago, but we are attracted by high-fat, sugary, more or less frivolous fad foods. Our cells cooperate with each other along the same lines set down by evolution in tree ferns of the Cretaceous period, but we find a new enemy somewhere in the world every decade, perhaps every year or month. We all have a similar tale to tell of deviations from the precise, complete, and almost perfect wisdom that our bodies follow.

Our wayward lapses point to a much larger pattern. To get back to the cell's wisdom, each of us needs to see that we are living the aftereffects of someone else's old choices. We were taught to follow a set of habits and beliefs that totally disregard the mystery of life. These beliefs are contained one inside the other like nested boxes:

There is a material world.
The material world is full of things, events, and people.

I am one of those people, and my status is no higher than that of
anyone else.

To find out who I am, I must explore the material world.

This set of beliefs is binding. It allows no room for soul-
searching, or even for the soul itself. Why bring the mystery of life
into a system that already knows what is real? But as convincing as
the material world looks, to the great embarrassment of modern science, no one has been able to prove that it is real. Ordinary people
don't focus on science, so this glaring problem is not well known. Yet
any neurologist will assure you that the brain offers no proof that the
outside world really exists and many hints that it doesn't.

All the brain does, in fact, is to receive continuous signals about
the body's state of chemical balance, temperature, and oxygen consumption, along with a crackling stream of nerve impulses. This
mass of raw data starts out as chemical bursts with attached electrical charges. These blips run up and down a tangled web of spidery
nerve cells, and once a signal reaches the brain, like a runner from the
edge of the Empire bringing a message to Rome, the cortex assem-
bles the raw data into even more complex arrangements of electrical
and chemical blips.

The cortex doesn't inform us about this never-ending data processing, which is all that is happening inside gray matter. Instead,
the cortex tells us about the world—it allows us to perceive sights,
sounds, tastes, smells, and textures—the whole array of creation. The
brain has pulled an enormous trick on us, a remarkable sleight of
hand, because there is no direct connection between the body's raw
data and our subjective sense of an outside world.

For all anyone knows, the entire outside world could be a dream.
When I'm in bed having a dream, I see a world of events just as
vivid as the waking world (for most of us, the other four senses are
scattered unevenly throughout our dreams, but some dreamers can

touch, taste, hear, and smell as accurately as they can while awake). But when I open my eyes in the morning, I know that these vivid events were all produced inside my head. I'd never make the mistake of falling for this trick because I already assume that dreams aren't real.

So does my brain dedicate one apparatus to making the dream world and another to the waking world? No, it doesn't. In terms of cerebral function, the dream mechanism doesn't flick off when I wake up. The same visual cortex in the rear of my skull allows me to see an object—a tree, a face, the sky—whether I am seeing it in memory, in a dream, in a photo, or standing before me. The locations of brain cell activity shift slightly from one to the other, which is why I can distinguish among a dream, a photo, and the real thing, yet the same fundamental process is constantly taking place. I am manufacturing a tree, a face, or the sky from what is actually a random tangle of spidery nerves shooting bursts of chemicals and electrical charges in my brain and all around my body. No matter how hard I try, I will never find a single pattern of chemicals and charges in the shape of a tree, a face, or any other shape. There is just a firestorm of electrochemical activity.

This embarrassing problem—that there is no way to prove the existence of an outside world—undermines the entire basis of materialism. Thus we arrive at the second spiritual secret: *You are not in the world; the world is in you.*

The only reason that rocks are solid is that the brain registers a flurry of electrical signals as touch; the only reason the sun shines is that the brain registers another flurry of electrical signals as sight. There is no sunlight in my brain, whose interior remains as dark as a limestone cavern no matter how bright it is outside.

Having said that the whole world is created in me, I immediately realize that you could say the same thing. Are you in my dream or am I in yours—or are we all trapped in some bizarre combination of each other's personal version of events? To me, this isn't a problem but the very heart of spirituality. Everyone is a creator. The mystery of how all these individual viewpoints somehow mesh, so that your world and mine can harmonize, is the very thing that makes people seek spiritual answers. For there is no doubt that reality is full of conflict but also full of harmony. It is very liberating to realize that as creators we generate every aspect, good or bad, of our experience. In this way, each of us is the center of creation.

People used to find these ideas very natural. Centuries ago the doctrine of one reality occupied center stage in spiritual life. Religions and peoples and traditions varied wildly, but there was universal agreement that the world is a seamless creation imbued with one intelligence, one creative design. Monotheism called the one reality God; India called it Brahman; China called it the Tao. By any name, every person existed within this infinite intelligence, and whatever we did on our own was part of creation's grand design. A person didn't have to become a spiritual seeker to find the one reality. Everybody's life already fit into it. The creator permeated each particle of creation equally, and the same divine spark animated life in all its forms.

Today we'd call this view mystical because it deals in invisible things. But if our ancestors had had access to microscopes, wouldn't they have seen concrete proof of their mysticism in the way cells behave? To believe in an all-embracing reality places everyone at the center of existence. The mystical symbol for this was a circle with a dot in the center, signifying that each individual (the dot) was secretly infinite (the circle). This is like the tiny cell whose central dot of DNA connects it to billions of years of evolution.

But is the concept of one reality mystical at all? Outside my window in winter I can usually spy at least one chrysalis dangling from a branch. Inside it a caterpillar has turned into a pupa that will emerge in spring as a butterfly. We are all familiar with this metamorphosis, having witnessed it as children (or by reading Eric Carle's *The Very Hungry Caterpillar*). But what goes on invisibly inside the chrysalis remains deeply mysterious. The caterpillar's organs and tissues dissolve into an amorphous, souplike state, only to reconstitute into the structure of a butterfly's body that bears no resemblance to a caterpillar at all.

Science has no idea why metamorphosis evolved. It is almost impossible to imagine that insects hit on it by chance—the chemical complexity of turning into a butterfly is incredible; thousands of steps are all minutely interconnected. (It's as if you dropped off a bicycle at the shop to be repaired, and when you came back the parts had become a Gulfstream jet.)

But we do have some idea about how this delicate chain of events is linked. Two hormones, one called *juvenile hormone,* the other *ecdysone,* regulate the process, which looks to the naked eye like a caterpillar dissolving into soup. These two hormones make sure that the cells moving from larva to butterfly know where they are going and how they are to change. Some cells are told to die; others digest themselves, while still others turn into eyes, antennae, and wings. This implies a fragile (and miraculous) rhythm that must remain in precise balance between creation and destruction. That rhythm, it turns out, depends on day length, which in turn depends on the earth's rotation around the sun. Therefore, a cosmic rhythm has been intimately connected to the birth of butterflies for millions of years.

Science concentrates on the molecules, but this is a striking example of intelligence at work, using molecules as a vehicle for its own intent. The intent in this case was to create a new creature without wasting old ingredients. (And if there is only one reality, we can't say, as science does, that day length *causes* the pupa's hormones to begin the metamorphosis into a butterfly. Day length and hormones come from the same creative source, weaving one reality. That source uses cosmic rhythms or molecules as it sees fit. Day length doesn't cause hormones to change any more than hormones cause the day to change—both are tied to a hidden intelligence that creates both at once. In a dream or a painting, a boy may hit a baseball, but his bat doesn't cause the ball to fly through the air. The whole dream or painting fits together seamlessly.)

Here is another example: Two chemicals called *actin* and *myosin* evolved eons ago to allow the muscles in insect wings to contract and relax. Thus, insects learned to fly. When one of these paired molecules is absent, wings will grow but they cannot flap and are therefore useless. Today, the same two proteins are responsible for the beating of the human heart, and when one is absent, the person's heartbeat is inefficient and weak, ultimately leading to heart failure.

Again, science marvels at the way molecules adapt over millions of years, but isn't there a deeper intent? In our hearts, we feel the impulse to fly, to break free of boundaries. Isn't that the same impulse nature expressed when insects began to take flight? The prolactin that generates milk in a mother's breast is unchanged from the prolactin that sends salmon upstream to breed, enabling them to cross from saltwater to fresh. The insulin in a cow is exactly the same as the insulin in an amoeba; both serve to metabolize carbohydrates, even though a cow is millions of times more complex than an amoeba. To believe in one reality that is totally interconnected isn't mystical at all, it turns out.

How, then, did the belief in one reality fall apart? There was another alternative, which also put each person at the center of his or her own world. But instead of being included, one feels alone and isolated, driven by personal desire rather than a shared life force or communion through the soul. This is the choice we call *ego,* although it has been called by other names, such as the pursuit of pleasure, the bondage of karma, and (if we resort to a religious vocabulary) banishment from paradise. So thoroughly does it permeate our culture, following your ego doesn't feel like a choice anymore. We've all been carefully trained since childhood in the ways of I, me, and mine. Competition teaches us that we have to fight for what we want. The threat of other egos, who feel as isolated and alone as we do, is ever present—our desires could be thwarted if someone else gets there first.

I don't have an ego-bashing agenda in mind here. Ego bashing looks for a villain whose actions keep people from finding happiness, which is the underlying reason why people suffer, why they never find their true self, God, or the soul. The ego, we are told, blinds us with its constant demands, its greed, selfishness, and insecurity. That is a common theme but a mistaken one, because throwing the ego into the dark, making it an enemy, only creates more division and fragmentation. If there is one reality, it must be all-inclusive. The ego can't be thrown out any more than desire can be thrown out.

The choice to live in separation—a choice no cell ever makes unless it becomes cancerous—gave rise to a certain strain of mythology. Every culture tells the story of a golden age buried in the dim past. This story of lost perfection debases human beings instead of exalting them. People told themselves that human nature must be innately flawed, that everyone wore the scars of sin, that God disapproved of his once-innocent children. A myth has the power to take a choice and make it seem like destiny. Separation took on a life of its own, but did the possibility of one reality ever really go away?

To embrace one reality again, we must accept that the world is in us. This is a spiritual secret based on the nature of the brain, which spends every second manufacturing the world. When your best friend calls you on the phone from Tibet, you take for granted that he is far away, yet the sound of his voice occurs as a sensation in your brain. If your friend shows up on your doorstep, his voice hasn't gotten any closer. It is still a sensation in the same part of your brain, and it will remain there after your friend leaves and his voice lingers inside you. When you look at a distant star, it too seems far away, yet it exists as a sensation in another part of your brain. So the star is in you. The same is true when you taste an orange or touch a velvet cloth or listen to Mozart—every possible experience is being manufactured inside yourself.

At this moment, ego-based life is thoroughly convincing, which is why no amount of pain and suffering drives people to abandon it. Pain hurts, but it doesn't show a way out. The debate on how to end war, for example, has proved totally futile because the instant I see myself as an isolated individual, I confront "them," the countless other individuals who want what I want.

Violence is built into the opposition of us versus them. "They" never go away and "they" never give up. They will always fight to protect their stake in the world. As long as you and I have a separate stake in the world, the cycle of violence will remain permanent. The dire results can be seen in the body, too. In a healthy body, every cell recognizes itself in every other cell. When this perception goes awry and certain cells become "the other," the body goes on an attack against itself. This state is known as an *auto-immune disorder,* of which rheumatoid arthritis and lupus are devastating examples. The violence of self against self is based entirely on a mistaken concept, and although medicine can bring some relief to the war-torn body, no cure can be achieved without correcting the mistaken concept first.

Getting serious about bringing violence to an end means giving up a personal stake in the world, once and for all. That alone will pluck violence out by the roots. This may sound like a shocking conclusion. One's immediate reaction is to say, "But I *am* my personal stake in the world." Fortunately, such isn't the case. The world is in you, not the other way around. This is what Christ meant when he taught that one should attain the kingdom of God first and worry about worldly things later, if at all. God owns everything by virtue of having created everything. If you and I are creating every perception that we take for reality, then we are allowed to own our creation as well.

Perception is the world; the world is perception.

In that key idea, the drama of us-versus-them collapses. We are all included in the only project that makes any difference: reality-making. To defend any outside thing—money, property, possessions, or status—makes sense only if those things are essential. But the material world is an aftereffect. Nothing in it is essential. The only personal stake worth having is the ability to create freely, with full awareness of how reality-making works.

I feel sympathetic to those who have examined the ego and found it so repugnant that they want to be without ego. But in the end, attacking the ego is just a subtle disguise for attacking yourself. Destroying the ego would serve no purpose even if it could be achieved. It is vital to keep our entire creative machinery intact. When you strip away its ugly, insecure, violent dreams, the ego is no longer ugly, insecure, and violent. It takes its natural place as part of the mystery.

The one reality has already revealed a deep secret: *Being a creator is more important than the whole world.* It's worth pausing for a moment to take that in. In fact, it is the world. Of all the liberating ideas that could change a person's life, this one is perhaps the most freeing. Yet to truly live it, to be a true creator, a great deal of conditioning needs to be broken down. No one remembers being told to believe in the material world. Yet somehow we've learned to accept ourselves as limited beings. The outside world must be far more powerful. It dictates the storyline, not you. The world comes first; you come a distant second.

The outside world will never produce any spiritual answers until you take on a new role as the manufacturer of reality. That feels strange at first, yet we can already see how a new set of beliefs is falling into place:

Everything I am experiencing reflects myself: Therefore I don't have to try and escape. There is nowhere to escape to, and as long as

I see myself as the creator of my reality, I wouldn't want to escape even if I could.

My life is part of every other life: My connection to all living things makes it impossible that I have enemies. I feel no need to oppose, resist, conquer, or destroy.

I have no need to control anyone or anything: I can affect change by transforming the only thing that I ever had control of in the first place, which is myself.

CHANGING YOUR REALITY TO ACCOMMODATE THE SECOND SECRET

To truly possess the second secret, begin to see yourself as a co-creator in everything that happens to you. One simple exercise is to sit wherever you are and look around. As your gaze falls on a chair, a picture, the color of the walls in your room, say to yourself, "This stands for me. This, too, stands for me." Let your awareness take in everything, and now ask yourself:

Do I see order or disorder?
Do I see my uniqueness?
Do I see how I really feel?
Do I see what I really want?

Some things in your environment will speak instantly to these questions while others won't. A bright, cheerfully painted apartment open to the light stands for a very different state of mind than a dark basement efficiency. Yet a cluttered desk piled high with papers could stand for quite a few things: inner disorder, fear of meeting one's obligations, accepting too much responsibility, ignoring mundane details, and so on. This inconsistency is valid because we each express and at the same time hide who we are. Some of the time you express who you are, while at other times you detach from your real feelings, deny them, or find outlets that feel socially acceptable. If that sofa was bought just because it was cheap and you decided to make do, if the wall color is white because you didn't care what color you looked at, if you're afraid to throw out a picture because your in-laws gave it to you as a present, you are still seeing symbols of how you feel. Without dwelling on details, it's possible to scan someone's personal space and fairly accurately discern if that person is satisfied or dissatisfied with life, has a strong or weak sense of personal identity, is a conformist or nonconformist, values order over chaos, feels optimistic or hopeless.

Now step into your social world. When you are with your family or friends, listen with your inner ear to what is going on. Ask yourself:

Do I hear happiness?
Does being with these people make me feel alive, alert?
Is there an undertone of fatigue?
Is this just a familiar routine, or are these people really respond-
ing to each other?

However you answer these questions, you are assessing your world and what is going on inside you. Other people, like the objects in your surroundings, are a mirror. Now turn on the evening news, and instead of watching it as if events are happening "out there," tune in personally. Ask yourself:

Does this world I see feel safe or unsafe?
Do I feel the fear and dismay of a disaster, or am I just being tit-
illated and entertained?
When the news is bad, am I still watching basically to be entertained?

> Which part of me does this program stand for? The part that
> dwells on one problem after another or the part that wants to
> find answers?

This exercise develops a new kind of awareness. You begin to
break the habit of seeing yourself as an isolated, separate entity. The
realization dawns that the whole world is actually nowhere but
inside you.

Exercise #2: Bringing Home the World

To say that you are a creator isn't the same as to say that your ego is.
The ego will always remain attached to your personality, and certainly your personality doesn't create everything around you.
Creation doesn't happen on that level. Let's see, then, if we can get
closer to the real creator inside you. We'll do this by meditating on
a rose.

Get a beautiful red rose and hold it in front of you. Inhale the fragrance and say to yourself, "Without me, this flower would have no
fragrance." Take in the glowing crimson color and say to yourself,
"Without me, this flower would have no color." Stroke the velvety
petals and say to yourself, "Without me, this flower would have no
texture." Realize that if you subtract yourself from any sensation—
sight, sound, touch, taste, smell—the rose would be nothing but
atoms vibrating in a void.

Now consider the DNA that is inside each cell of the rose.
Visualize the billions of atoms strung along a double helix and say to
yourself, "My DNA is looking at the DNA in this flower. The experience is not an observer looking at an object. DNA in one form is looking at DNA in another form." Now see the DNA begin to shimmer
and turn into invisible vibrations of energy. Say to yourself, "The rose
has vanished into its primal energy. I have vanished into my primal
energy. Now only one energy field is looking at another energy field."

Finally, see the boundary between your energy and the rose's energy fade as one set of waves merges into another, like ocean waves rising and falling on the vast surface of an endless sea. Say to yourself, "All energy comes from one source and returns to it. When I look at a rose, a tiny flicker of infinity is rising from the source to experience itself."

Having followed this trail, you have arrived at what is truly real: An infinite, silent energy field flickered for an instant, experiencing an object (the rose) and a subject (you the observer) without going anywhere. Awareness simply took a look at one aspect of its eternal beauty. Its only motive was to create a moment of joy. You and the rose stood at opposite poles of that moment, yet there was no separation. A single creative stroke took place, fusing you both.

✽

FOUR PATHS LEAD TO UNITY

ALL THE SPIRITUAL SECRETS from this point on, meaning the vast majority, depend on your accepting the existence of one reality. If you still think of it as a pet idea held by someone else, your experience of life won't change. One reality isn't an idea—it is a doorway into a completely new way to participate in life. Imagine a passenger on an airplane who doesn't know that flight exists. As the plane takes off he panics, thinking such thoughts as "What's holding us up? What if this plane is too heavy? Air weighs nothing, and this whole plane is made of steel!" Thrown back on his own perceptions, the panicked passenger loses all sense of being in control; he is trapped in an experience that could be leading to disaster.

In the cockpit the pilot feels more in control because he's been trained to fly. He knows the aircraft; he understands the plane's controls that he works. Therefore he has no reason to panic, even though in the back of his mind the danger of mechanical failure is always present. Disaster could occur, but that is out of his control.

Now move on to the designer of jet planes, who can build any craft he wants based on the principle of flight. He occupies a position of greater control than the pilot because if he kept on experimenting with various designs, he could come up with a plane that is incapable of crashing (perhaps some kind of glider with an airfoil that never stalls, no matter what angle of dive the plane goes into).

This progression from passenger to pilot to designer is symbolic of a spiritual journey. The passenger is trapped in the world of the five senses. He can perceive flight only as impossible because when steel is compared to air, it only seems capable of falling through it. The pilot knows the principles of flight, which transcend the five senses by going to a deeper law of nature (the Bernoulli principle), which dictates that air flowing over a curved surface creates lift. The designer transcends even further by coaxing the laws of nature to arrive at an intended effect. In other words, he is closest to the source of reality, acting not as a victim of the five senses or a passive participant in natural law but as a co-creator with nature.

You can take this journey yourself. It is more than symbolic because the brain, which is already manufacturing every sight, sound, touch, taste, and smell that you experience, is a quantum machine. Its atoms are in direct contact with the laws of nature, and through the magic of consciousness, when you have a desire, your brain is sending a signal to the very source of natural law. The simplest definition of consciousness is awareness; the two are synonymous. One time at a business conference an executive came up to me demanding a definition of *consciousness* that was practical and concrete. At first I wanted to reply that consciousness can't be defined concretely, but I found myself blurting out, "Consciousness is the potential for all creation." His face brightened as he suddenly got it. The more consciousness you have, the more potential you have to create. Pure consciousness, because it underlies everything, is pure potential.

You need to ask yourself this question: Do you want to be a victim of the five senses or a co-creator? Here are how the options look.

ON THE WAY TO CREATION

- **Depending on the five senses:** Separation, duality, ego-based, subject to fear, detached from the source, limited in time and space.

- **Depending on natural law:** In control, less subject to fear, taps into natural resources, inventive, understanding, explores the reaches of time and space.

- **Depending on consciousness:** Creative, intimate with natural law, close to the source, boundaries dissolve, intentions turn into results, beyond time and space.

Awareness is all that changes in the journey from separation to the one reality. When you depend on your five senses, you are aware of the physical world as primary reality. In such a world you must come second because you see yourself as a solid object made up of atoms and molecules. The only role your awareness has is to look upon the world "out there."

The five senses are extremely deceptive. They tell us that the sun rises in the east and sets in the west, that the earth is flat, that an object made of steel couldn't possibly be held up by air. The next stage of awareness depends upon laws of nature that are arrived at by thinking and experimenting. The observer is no longer a victim of deception. He can figure out the law of gravity using mathematics and thought experiments. (Newton didn't have to sit under a tree and have an actual apple fall on his head—he could perform a thought experiment using images and the numbers that match those images. This was the process he followed, as did Einstein by imagining how relativity worked.)

When the human brain considers the laws of nature, the material world is still "out there" to be explored. More power is gained over nature, but if this level of awareness was the ultimate one (as many scientists think it is), utopia would be a technological triumph.

However, the brain can't set itself aside forever. The laws of nature that keep airplanes in the air also apply to every electron in the brain. Eventually someone has to ask, "Who am I who is doing all this thinking?" That's the question that leads to pure awareness. For if you empty the brain of all thoughts (as in a state of meditation), awareness turns out not to be empty, void, and passive. Beyond the limits of time and space, one process—and only one—is taking place. Creation is creating itself, using consciousness as its modeling clay. Consciousness turns into things in the objective world, into experiences in the subjective world. Break any experience down to its most basic element, and what you get are invisible ripples in the quantum field; break down any object into its most basic element, and what you get is also a ripple in the quantum field. There is no difference, and by a stroke of supreme magic, the human brain doesn't have to stand outside the creative process. Just by paying attention and having a desire, you flip on the switch of creation.

You flip it on, that is, if you know what you're doing. The victim of the five senses (pre-scientific man) and the explorer of the laws of nature (scientists and philosophers) are just as creative as someone experiencing pure awareness (sages, saints, shamans, siddhas, sorcerers—pick any label you want). But they believe in limitations that are self-imposed. And because they do, those limitations turn into reality. The glory of the spiritual journey is the same as its irony: You acquire full power only by realizing that you have been using that power all along to thwart yourself. You are potentially the prisoner, the jailer, and the hero who opens the prison, all rolled into one.

Instinctively we knew this all along. In fairy tales there is a magical connection between victims and heroes. The frog knows he is a prince, needing only the magic touch to regain his true status. Most fairy tales put the victim in peril, unable to break the spell until the magic is delivered from outside. The frog needs a kiss; the sleeping princess needs someone to break through the wall of thorns; Cinderella needs a fairy godmother with a magic wand. Fairy tales symbolize a belief in magic that wells up from the most ancient parts of our brain, but they also lament that we are not masters of this magic.

This dilemma has frustrated everyone who has tried to embrace the one reality. Even when wisdom is gained and you realize that your own brain is producing everything around you, finding the control switch to creation is elusive. But there is a way. Behind any experience is an experiencer who knows what is happening. When I find a way to stand where the experiencer is standing, I will be at the still point around which the whole world turns. Getting there is a process that starts here and now.

Every experience comes to us in one of four ways: as a feeling, a thought, an action, or simply a sense of being. At unexpected moments the experiencer is more present in these four things than usual. When that happens, we feel a change, a slight difference from our ordinary reality. Here is a list of such subtle changes taken from a notepad I kept by my side for several weeks:

FEELINGS

A lightness in my body.

A streaming or flowing sensation in my body.

A sense that all is well, that I am at home in the world.

A feeling of complete peacefulness.

A sensation of coming to rest, as if a speeding car has glided to a halt.

A feeling of landing in a soft place where I am safe.

A feeling that I am not what I seem to be, that I have been playing a part that isn't the real me.

A feeling that something lies beyond the sky or behind the mirror.

THINKING

"I know more than I think I do."

"I need to find out what's real."

"I need to find out who I really am."

My mind is becoming less restless; it wants to calm down.

My inner voices have become very quiet.

My internal dialogue has suddenly stopped.

ACTIONS

I suddenly sense that my actions are not my own.

I sense a greater power acting through me.

My actions seem to symbolize who I am and why I'm here.

I am acting out of complete integrity.

I gave up control and what I wanted simply came to me.

I gave up the struggle, and instead of falling apart, things got better.

My actions are part of a plan I can barely glimpse, but I know it must exist.

BEING

I realize that I am cared for.

I realize that my life has purpose, that I matter.

I sense that random events are not random but form subtle patterns.

I see that I am unique.

I realize that life has the ability to run itself.

I feel drawn to the center of things.

I realize with wonder that life is infinitely worthwhile.

This may seem like a very abstract list because everything on it is about awareness. I didn't record the thousands of other thoughts, feelings, and actions that centered on outside things. Of course, like everyone else, I was thinking about my next appointment or rushing to it, feeling harried in traffic, being happy or out of sorts, confused or certain, focused or distracted. All of that is like the contents of a mental suitcase. People stuff their suitcases with thousands of things. Yet awareness is not a suitcase, nor is it the things you stuff inside.

Awareness is just itself—pure, alive, alert, silent, and full of potential. Sometimes you come close to experiencing that pure state, and at these times one of the hints I've listed, or something similar, comes to the surface instead of lying hidden out of sight. Some hints are palpable; they arise as undeniable sensations in the body. Others arise at a subtle level that is difficult to verbalize: a shiver of *something* unexpectedly catches your attention. If you notice even one such hint, you have in your hand a thread that could lead beyond thought, feeling, or action. If there is only one reality, every clue must lead eventually to the same place where the laws of creation operate freely, which is awareness itself.

Once you start out with a promising hint, how can you wrest free from the ego's grip? The ego fiercely protects its view of the world, and we've all experienced how wispy and fleeting any experience can be when it doesn't fit our ingrained belief system. Sir Kenneth Clark, the renowned English art historian, recounts in his autobiography about an epiphany in a church when he suddenly realized, with total clarity, that an all-embracing presence was filling him. He sensed beyond thought a reality that was sublime, filled with light, loving, and sacred.

At that moment he had a choice: He could pursue this transcendental reality or he could go back to art. He chose art, without apology. Art, even if it fell far short of higher reality, was Clark's earthly love. He was choosing one infinity over another—the infinity of beautiful objects over the infinity of invisible awareness. (There is a witty cartoon showing a fingerpost standing at the fork of a trail. One sign points toward "God," the other toward "Discussions about

God." In this case the signs could be changed to "God" and "Pictures of God.")

Many other people have made similar choices. In order to displace the physical world you already know, a hint must expand. The threads of experience must weave a new pattern because, as separate strands, they are too fragile to compete with the familiar drama of pleasure and pain that grips all of us.

Consider the list again. The boundaries between the categories are blurry. There is only the slightest difference between *feeling* that I am safe, for example, and *knowing* that I am safe. From this I can proceed to *acting* as if I am safe until finally I realize, without a doubt, that my whole existence has been safe since I was born: I *am* safe. In practical terms, this is what it means to weave a whole new pattern. If I take any other item from the list, I can weave similar interconnections. As I draw thought, feeling, action, and being together, the experiencer becomes more real; I am learning to put myself in his place. Then I can test this new reality to see if it has enough strength to replace an older, outworn picture of myself.

You might want to pause for a moment and do just that: Choose any item that speaks to you—a sensation or thought you can remember having—and connect it to the other three categories. Let's say you pick "I see that I am unique." Uniqueness means that there is no one else who is exactly like you. What feeling would go with that realization? Perhaps a feeling of strength and self-esteem, or a sensation of being like a flower with its own unique scent, form, and color. There is also the sensation of standing out from the crowd and being proud that you do. The thought might then come, "I don't have to imitate anybody else." With this thought you might begin to feel free of other people's opinions about you. From this, a desire arises to act with integrity, to show the world that you know who you are. Thus, from one tiny sensation a whole new pattern emerges; you have found the path of expanded awareness. If you pursue a momentary glimpse of awareness, you will see how quickly it expands; a single thread leads to a complex tapestry. Yet this metaphor cannot explain how to change reality itself. To master pure awareness, you must learn how to live it.

When an experience is so powerful that it motivates people to change the whole pattern of their lives, we call that a breakthrough, or an epiphany. The value of an epiphany doesn't lie just in some new or exciting insight. You might be walking down the street and pass a stranger. Your eyes meet, and for some reason there is a connection. It isn't sexual or romantic or even a suspicion that this person could mean something in your life. Instead, the epiphany is that you *are* that stranger—your experiencer merges with his. Call this a feeling or a thought, it doesn't matter which—it's the sudden expansion that counts. You are flung outside your narrow boundaries, if only for a moment, and that makes all the difference. You have tasted a hidden dimension. Compared to the habit of shutting yourself behind the walls of ego, this new dimension feels freer and lighter. You have a sense that your body can't contain you anymore.

Another example: When you watch a young child who is playing with complete focus and yet totally carefree, it's hard not to feel a tug. Doesn't the child's innocence seem palpable at that moment? Can't you feel in yourself—or yearn to feel—the same delight in play? Doesn't the child's tiny body seem as fragile as a soap bubble and yet bursting with life itself, something immense, eternal, never to be defeated? In a fascinating text called the *Shiva Sutras,* which dates back centuries in India, one can find similar epiphanies. Each one is a sudden glimpse of freedom in which the underlying experiencer is directly confronted, without interference. One looks at a beautiful woman and suddenly one sees beauty itself. Or one looks at the sky and suddenly one sees an infinity beyond.

No one else, however much you love and adore the person, sees the true significance of your private epiphanies. The secret belongs to you, with you, in you. In the title *Shiva Sutra,* the word *Shiva* means "God" and the word *Sutra* means "thread," so quite deliberately the reader is being shown tiny threads that lead back to the eternal source.

There is a wider context for the *Shiva Sutras,* which requires following the path that is opened up by an epiphany. In the Vedic tradition, each person can choose four paths that arise from feeling, thinking, acting, and being. Each path is called a *Yoga,* the Sanskrit word for "union," because unity—merging with one reality—was the goal. Over the ages, the four Yogas have come to define specific paths that suit the kind of temperament a seeker has, although in truth you can follow several or all at once:

Bhakti Yoga leads to unity by loving God.
Karma Yoga leads to unity through selfless action.
Gyana Yoga leads to unity through knowledge.
Raj Yoga leads to unity through meditation and renunciation.

Literally translated, the fourth path, Raj Yoga, means "the royal way to union." What makes it royal is a belief that meditation transcends the other three paths. But the fourth path is also inclusive: By following it you are actually following all four at once. Your meditations go directly to the essence of your being. That essence is what love of God, selfless action, and knowledge are trying to reach.

It's not necessary to think of the four paths as being Eastern. These Yogas were the original seeds, the means that brought unity within reach. Everyone has feelings, so everyone can be on the path of feeling. The same is true for thinking, acting, and being. So the vision of Yoga is simply that unity is possible for anyone, starting from wherever you happen to be. Indeed, unity is secretly present in every moment of daily life. Nothing can happen to me that is outside the one reality; nothing is wasted or random in the cosmic design.

Let's look at how each path is actually lived:

Feeling points the way whenever you experience and express love. On this path your personal emotions expand to become all-encompassing. Love of self and family merges into love of humanity. In its highest expression, your love is so powerful that it calls upon God to show himself (or herself) to you. The yearning heart finds ultimate peace by uniting with the heart of creation.

Thinking points the way whenever your mind stops being restless and speculative. On this path, you silence your internal dialogue in order to find clarity and stillness. It takes clarity for your mind to see that it doesn't have to be so driven. Thinking can turn into knowing, which is to say wisdom. With greater clarity your intellect looks into any problem and sees the solution. As your knowingness expands, personal questions fade. What your mind really wants to know is the mystery of existence. Questions knock on the door of eternity, at which point only the Creator can answer them for you. The fulfillment of this path comes when your mind merges with the mind of God.

Action points the way whenever you surrender. On this path your ego's control over action is loosened. Your actions stop being motivated by selfish wants and wishes. At the beginning, it is inescapable that you will be acting for yourself because, even if you try to be completely selfless, you will be earning personal satisfaction. In time, however, action detaches from the ego. Doing becomes motivated by a force outside yourself. This universal force is called Dharma in Sanskrit. The path of action is summed up in a phrase: Karma gives way to Dharma. In other words, personal attachment to your own actions is turned into nonattachment through performing God's actions. This path reaches its fulfillment when your surrender is so complete that God runs everything you do.

Being points the way whenever you cultivate a self beyond ego. At the outset the sense of "I" is attached to fragments of your real identity. "I" is an accumulation of everything that has happened to you since you were born. This shallow identity gets exposed as an illusion, a mask that hides a much greater "I" existing in everyone. Your real identity is a sense of existence pure and simple, which we'll call "I am." All creatures share the same "I am," and fulfillment occurs when your being embraces so much that God is also included in your sense of being alive. Unity is a state in which nothing is left out of "I am."

Yoga is seen in the West as a renunciant's path, a way of life that demands giving up family and possessions. Wandering yogis with their begging bowls, of the kind that used to be seen in every village in India, symbolize such a life. But outer trappings don't signify renunciation, which happens on the inside no matter how much or how little you possess materially. Internally, a crucial decision is made: *I am starting over.* In other words, you renounce your old perceptions, not your possessions.

When your heart grows sick of the violence and divisiveness in the world, starting over is the only choice. You stop looking at the reflections and turn instead to the source. The universe, like any mirror, is neutral. It reflects back whatever is in front of it, without judgment or distortion. If you can trust that, then you have taken the crucial step of renunciation. You've renounced the belief that the outer world has power over you. As with everything else on the path to unity, living this truth is what will make it true.

CHANGING YOUR REALITY TO ACCOMMODATE THE THIRD SECRET

Finding a path back to your source is a matter of letting life settle down to where it wants to be. There are gross and subtle levels of every experience, and the subtler levels are more sensitive, awake, and meaningful than the gross. As an exercise, begin to observe when you touch upon subtle levels in your own awareness. Notice how these feel compared to the grosser levels. For example:

> To love someone is subtler than to resent or push the person away.
> To accept someone is subtler than to criticize the individual.
> To promote peace is subtler than to promote anger and violence.
> To see someone without judgment is subtler than to criticize the person.

If you let yourself feel it, the subtler side of each experience puts the mind at ease, decreases stress, and results in less restless thinking and less pressure at the emotional level. Subtle experience is quiet and harmonious. You feel settled; you aren't in conflict with anyone else. There is no overblown drama or even any need for it.

Once you have identified it, begin to favor the subtle side of your life. Value this level of awareness—only if you value it will it grow. If you favor the grosser levels instead, the world will reflect your perception back to you: It will always remain divisive, disturbing, stressful, and threatening. The choice is yours to make at the level of consciousness because, in the infinite diversity of creation, every perception gives rise to a world that mirrors it.

Exercise #2: Meditation

Any experience that brings you into contact with the silent level of awareness can be called meditation. You may have spontaneously hit upon a routine that allows you to experience a deep settling in your mind. If you haven't yet, then you might adopt one of the more formal meditation practices that appear in every spiritual tradition. The simplest, perhaps, is breathing meditation, as follows:

Sit quietly with your eyes closed in a room with the lights low and no distractions from the telephone or knocks at the door. Shut your eyes for a few minutes; then become aware of your breathing. Let your attention follow your breath as it gently, naturally draws inward. Do the same as the breath flows outward. Don't make any attempt to breathe with a certain rhythm and don't try to make your breath deep or shallow.

By following your breath you are aligning yourself with the mind-body connection, the subtle coordination of thought and *Prana,* the subtle energy contained in the breath. Some people find it easier to stay with their breathing if they repeat a sound: one syllable for the out breath, one for the inner. *Ah-Hum* is a traditional sound useful for this purpose. (You can also adopt the seed mantras or ritual sounds as described in any text on Eastern spiritual teachings.)

Perform this meditation for 10 to 20 minutes twice a day. You will become aware of your body relaxing. Since most people are storing massive amounts of fatigue and stress, you may even fall asleep. Don't worry about this, or about any sensation or thought that crops up as your mind grows quieter. Rely on the body's natural tendency to release stress. This is a gentle meditation that has no negative side effects or dangers as long as you are healthy. (If you feel pain anywhere or a repeated sense of discomfort, these may be symptoms of undiagnosed illness; in that case, should such feelings persist, you need to ask for medical help.)

The relaxing effect will continue, yet you will also begin to notice that you are more self-aware. You may gain a sudden insight or inspiration. You may start to feel more centered; sudden spurts of energy or alertness may occur. These effects vary from person to person, so be open to whatever comes. The overall purpose of meditation is the same for everyone, however: You are learning to relate to awareness itself, the purest level of experience.

❀

WHAT YOU SEEK,
YOU ALREADY ARE

WHEN I TURNED TWENTY-ONE as a medical student in New Delhi I had my choice of two kinds of friends. The materialistic kind got out of bed at noon and went to all-night parties where everyone drank Coca-Cola and danced to Beatles records. They had discovered cigarettes and women, perhaps even bootleg liquor, which was much cheaper than imported Scotch. The spiritual kind got up at dawn to go to temple—about the time the materialists were staggering home with hangovers—and they ate rice out of a bowl and drank water or tea, usually out of the same bowl.

It didn't seem strange at the time that all the materialists were Indians and all the spiritual types were Westerners. The Indians couldn't wait to leave home and go someplace where Coca-Cola, good tobacco, and legal whiskey were cheap and plentiful. The Westerners kept asking where the real holy men were in India, the kind who could levitate and heal lepers by touching them. As it happened, I ran with the materialists, who were all around me in class. Nobody who was actually born in India ever saw himself the other way, as a seeker.

Today I wouldn't have two types to choose from—everyone around me seems to be a seeker. In my mind, *seeking* is another word for chasing after something. My Indian classmates had the easier chase because it doesn't take much to get money and material things, whereas the spiritual types from the West almost never found their holy men. I used to think that the problem was due to how rare holy men actually are; now I realize that what defeated their thirst for a higher life was tied up in the act of seeking itself. Tactics that will successfully get you whiskey and Beatles records fail miserably when you chase holiness.

The spiritual secret that applies here is this: *What you seek, you already are.* Your awareness has its source in unity. Instead of seeking outside yourself, go to the source and realize who you are.

Seeking is a word often applied to the spiritual path, and many people are proud to call themselves seekers. Often, they are the same people who once chased too hard after money, sex, alcohol, or work. With the same addictive intensity they now hope to find God, the soul, the higher self. The problem is that seeking begins with a false assumption. I don't mean the assumption that materialism is corrupt and spirituality is pure. Yes, materialism can become all-consuming, but that's not the really important point. Seeking is doomed because it is a chase that takes you outside yourself. Whether the object is God or money makes no real difference. Productive seeking requires that you throw out all assumptions that there is a prize to be won. This means acting without hope of rising to some ideal self, hope being a wish that you'll get somewhere better than the place you started from. You are starting from yourself, and it's the self that contains all the answers. So you have to give up on the idea that you must go from A to B. There is no linear path when the goal isn't somewhere else. You must also discard fixed judgments about high and low, good and evil, holy and profane. The one reality includes everything in its tangle of experiences, and what we are trying to find is the experiencer who is present no matter what experience you are having.

Looking at the people who race around trying to be models of goodness, someone coined the apt phrase "spiritual materialism," the transfer of values that work in the material world over to the spiritual world.

SPIRITUAL MATERIALISM

Pitfalls of the Seeker

Knowing where you're going.
Struggling to get there.
Using someone else's map.
Working to improve yourself.
Setting a timetable.
Waiting for a miracle.

There's no better way to be a genuine seeker than to avoid these pitfalls.

● *Don't know where you're going.* Spiritual growth is spontaneous. The big events come along unexpectedly, and so do the small ones. A single word can open your heart; a single glance can tell you who you really are. Awakening doesn't happen according to the plan. It's much more like putting together a jigsaw puzzle without knowing the finished picture in advance. The Buddhists have a saying, "If you meet the Buddha on the path, kill him," which means if you're following a spiritual script written in advance, bury it. All you can imagine in advance are images, and images are never the same as the goal.

• *Don't struggle to get there.* If there were a spiritual payoff at the end of the trail, like a pot of gold or the key to heaven, everyone would work as hard as possible for the reward. Any struggle would be worth it. But does it help a two-year-old to struggle to become three? No, because the process of child development unfolds from within. You don't get a paycheck; you turn into a new person. The same is true for spiritual unfolding. It happens just as naturally as childhood development, but on the plane of awareness rather than in the realm of physiology.

• *Don't follow someone else's map.* There was a time when I was certain that deep meditation using one specific mantra for the rest of my life was the key to reaching enlightenment. I was following a map laid down thousands of years ago by venerable sages who belonged to India's greatest spiritual tradition. But caution is always required: If you follow someone else's map, you could be training yourself in a fixed way of thinking. Fixed ways, even those devoted to spirit, are not the same as being free. You should glean teachings from all directions, keeping true to those that bring progress yet remaining open to changes in yourself.

• *Don't make this a self-improvement project.* Self-improvement is real. People get stuck in bad places that they can learn to get out of. Depression, loneliness, and insecurity are tangible experiences that can be improved. But if you seek to reach God or enlightenment because you want to stop being depressed or anxious, if you want greater self-esteem or less loneliness, your search may never end. This area of understanding isn't cut-and-dried. Some people feel tremendously self-improved as their awareness expands; but it takes a strong sense of self to confront the many obstacles and challenges that lie on the path. If you feel weak or fragile, you may feel weaker and more fragile when you confront the shadow energies within. Expanded awareness comes at a price—you have to give up your limitations—and for anyone who feels victimized, that limitation is often so stubborn that spiritual progress becomes very slow. To the extent that you feel any deep conflict inside yourself, a large hurdle stands before you on the path. The wise thing is to seek help at the level where the problem exists.

- *Don't set yourself a timetable.* I've met countless people who gave up on spirituality because they didn't reach their goals fast enough. "I gave it ten years. What can I do? Life is only so long. I'm moving on." More likely they devoted just one year or a month to being on the path, and then the weekend warriors fell away, discouraged by lack of results. The best way to avoid disappointment is not to set a deadline in the first place, although many people find this difficult to do without losing motivation. But motivation was never going to get them there in the first place. Discipline is involved, no doubt, in remembering to meditate regularly, to keep up Yoga class, to read inspiring texts, and to keep your vision before you. Getting into the spiritual habit requires a sense of dedication. But unless the vision is unfolding every day, you will inevitably get distracted. Rather than a timetable, give yourself support for spiritual growth. This can be in the form of a personal teacher, a discussion group, a partner who shares the path with you, regular retreats, and keeping a daily journal. You will be much less likely to fall prey to disappointment.

- *Don't wait for a miracle.* It really doesn't matter how you define *miracle*—whether it is the sudden appearance of perfect love, a cure for a life-threatening disease, anointment from a great spiritual leader, or permanent and everlasting bliss. A miracle is letting God do all the work; it separates the supernatural world from this world, with the expectation that one day the supernatural world will notice you. Since there is only one reality, your task is to break through boundaries of division and separation. Watching and waiting for a miracle keeps the boundaries up. You are ever at a remove from God, connected to him by wishful thinking.

If you can avoid these pitfalls of spiritual materialism, you will be much less tempted to chase after an impossible goal. The chase began because people came to believe that God, disapproving of what he sees in us, expects us to adopt a certain ideal. It seems impossible to imagine a God, however loving, who doesn't get disappointed, angry, vengeful, or disgusted with us when we fall short. The most spiritual figures in history were not totally good, however, but totally human. They accepted and forgave; they lacked judgment. I think the highest forgiveness is to accept that creation is thoroughly tangled, with every possible quality given some outlet for expression. People need to accept once and for all that there is only one life and each of us is free to shape it through the choices we make. Seeking can't get anyone out of the tangle because *everything* is tangled up. The only thing that will ever be pure and pristine is your own awareness, once you sort it out.

It's much easier to keep up the fight between good and evil, holy and profane, us and them. But as awareness grows, these opposites begin to calm down in their clashes, and something else emerges— a world you feel at home in. The ego did you a terrible disservice by throwing you into a world of opposites. Opposites always conflict— that's the only way they know—and who can feel at home in the middle of a fight? Awareness offers an alternative beyond the fray.

Last night in bed, I was dreaming. The usual kinds of dream images were passing back and forth; I don't remember much what they were. All at once I became aware of the sound of breathing in my dream. After a second I realized that it was my wife, who was moving in her sleep beside me. I knew that I was hearing her, and yet I also knew that I was dreaming at the same time. For a few seconds I was in both worlds, and then I woke up.

Sitting up in bed, I had the strange sensation that it was no longer important that a dream isn't real. Being awake is more real than a dream only because we have agreed that it is. Actually, the sound of my wife breathing is in my head, whether I am dreaming or not. How, then, could I tell one from the other? *Someone else must be watching.* An observer was aware without getting caught up in being awake, asleep, or dreaming. Most of the time I am so caught up in waking, sleeping, and dreaming that I have no other perspective. The silent observer is the simplest version of me, the one that just is.

If you strip away all the distractions of life, something yet remains that is you. This version of yourself doesn't have to think or dream; it doesn't need sleep to feel rested. There is real joy in finding this version of yourself because it is already at home. It lives above the fray, totally untouched by the war of opposites. When people say that they are seeking, it's this level of themselves that is calling to them in its silent, untroubled way. Seeking is really just a way of winning yourself back.

But to win yourself back you have to get as close to zero as possible. At its very core, reality is pure existence. Meet yourself there and you will be able to create anything in existence. The "I am" contains all that is needed for making a world, even though by itself it consists of nothing but a silent witness.

You've already undertaken the exercise of looking at a rose and breaking it down from the level of a physical object to the level of energy vibrating in empty space. The other side of that exercise consisted of seeing that your brain can also be understood the same way. So when you are seeing a rose, is nothing looking at nothing?

So it would seem, but the real phenomenon is more amazing: You are looking at yourself. One part of your awareness, which you call yourself, is gazing upon itself in the form of a rose. There is no solid core to either the object or the observer. There is no person inside your head, only a swirl of water, salt, sugar, and a handful of other chemicals like potassium and sodium. This whirlpool of a brain is always flowing, and thus every experience is swept along in currents and eddies as swiftly as a mountain stream. So, where is the silent observer located if not in my brain? Neurologists have found locations for all kinds of mental states. No matter what a person is experiencing—depression, elation, creativity, hallucination, amnesia, paralysis, sexual longing, or anything else—the brain displays a signature pattern of activity scattered across various locations. Yet there is no location or pattern for the person having these experences. The person could be nowhere, at least nowhere that science will ever spot.

This is a cause for incredible excitement because, if the real you isn't inside your head, you have been set free, like awareness itself. This freedom is limitless. You can create anything because you are in every atom of creation. Wherever your awareness wants to go, matter must follow. You *do* come first after all and the universe second.

I can hear the cries of outrage from those who claim that today's worshippers think they are larger than God, that instead of obeying his laws they arrogantly want to define life any way they choose. There is some truth to this criticism, but it must be put into context. Imagine an infant who has been crawling for several months and who suddenly finds that there's a new mode of travel called walking. Everyone has watched a toddler find his legs—the baby's face shows a combination of unsteadiness and determination, insecurity and joy. "Can I do this?" "Should I fall back down and crawl, the way I know how to do?" What you're reading in a baby's face is exactly the same tangled experience of anyone caught at a spiritual crossroads. In both cases, everything is on the move in a new way. The brain is motivating the body; the body is bringing new information to the brain; unexpected actions begin to emerge from nowhere; and even though the whole mixture feels scary, a certain exhilaration drives us forward. "I don't know where I'm going, but I have to get there."

All experience takes place within the bubbling cauldron of creation. Every moment of life sweeps the body along in an uncertain balance of mind, emotions, perceptions, behavior, and outside events. Your attention gets pulled here and there. In a moment of awakening, the brain is just as confused, joyful, insecure, uneasy, and astonished as a baby finding his legs. But at the level of the witness, this confused mix is utterly clear: *It's all one thing.* Look at the baby again. As he lurches across the floor, the whole world totters with him. There's no steady place to stand, no way of saying, "I am in control. This is going to turn out the way I want it to." The baby has no choice but to plunge his whole being into a world that is bursting into new dimensions.

Can anyone live this way, plunging into new dimensions, all the time? No, stability must be found. Since childhood, all of us have found a stable point through the ego. We imagine a fixed "I" who is in control, at least as much as possible. But there is another, far more stable point of stability: the witness.

MEETING THE SILENT WITNESS

How to Seek Within

1. Follow the flow of awareness.
2. Don't resist what's happening inside.

3. Open yourself to the unknown.

4. Don't censor or deny what you feel.

5. Reach beyond yourself.

6. Be genuine, speak your truth.

7. Let the center be your home.

Follow the flow: The phrase "follow your bliss" has become a maxim for many people. The principle behind the maxim is that whatever brings a person deepest joy is a reliable guide to follow into the future. An even more reliable guide is to follow your awareness as it grows. Sometimes awareness doesn't equate with joy or bliss. You may be aware of a hidden need to feel grief or a nagging sense of unease or discontent with the limitations of your present life. Most people don't follow these signs. They search for outside sources of happiness, and they think their bliss comes from them. If you follow your awareness, however, you will find that it cuts a path through time and space. Awareness cannot unfold without also unfolding outside events that mirror it. Thus, desire and purpose are linked—if you follow your desire, the purpose reveals itself. There is a flow that links disconnected events, and *you are this flow.* When you were a child, the flow took you from one stage of development to the next; as an adult, it can do the same. No one can predict your next step of unfoldment, including yourself. But if you are willing to follow the flow, the path will certainly lead you closer to the silent witness, who resides at the source of all your desires.

Don't resist what's happening: It's impossible to be new and old at the same time, yet we all wish we could stay the way we are while changing in ways we desire. This is a perfect formula for getting stuck. To seek who you are, you have to let go of old images about yourself. Whether you like yourself or not is irrelevant. Someone with high self-esteem and proud accomplishments is still caught up in the battle of opposites—in fact, such people usually think they are

winning the battle for the "good" side. The part of yourself that has
found peace from all battles is the witness. If you ask to meet the witness, be prepared. Long-held habits centered on winning and losing,
being accepted or rejected, feeling in control or scattered, will begin
to change. Don't resist this change—you are shedding the trappings
of ego and moving to a new sense of self.

Open yourself to the unknown: This whole book, being about
the mystery of life, returns to the unknown many times. Who you
think you are is not real but a concoction of past events, desires, and
memories. This concoction has a life of its own—it motors forward
through time and space experiencing only those things that it
knows. A new experience isn't really new; it's just a slight twist on
very familiar sensations. To open yourself to the unknown means cutting the ground out from under your familiar reactions and habits.
Notice how often the same words come out of your mouth, the same
likes and dislikes dictate what you do with your time, the same people fill your life with routine. All of this familiarity is like a shell.
The unknown is outside the shell, and to encounter it, you have to
be willing to welcome it in.

Don't censor or deny what you feel: On the surface, everyday
life has become much more comfortable than ever before. Yet people
still lead lives of quiet desperation. The source of this desperation is
repression, a sense that you cannot be what you want to be, cannot
feel what you want to feel, cannot do what you want to do. A creator
should never be trapped in this way. No authority looms over you to
enforce repression; it is entirely self-enforced. Any part of yourself
that you cannot face puts a barrier between you and reality. Yet emotions are entirely private. Only you know how you feel, and when
you stop censoring your emotions, the effect goes far beyond feeling
better. Your aim is not to experience only positive emotions. The
road to freedom is not through feeling good; it is through feeling
true to yourself. We all owe emotional debts to the past, in the form

of feelings we couldn't allow ourselves to express. The past isn't over as long as these debts go unpaid. You don't have to return to the person who made you angry or afraid, with the intention of revising how the past turned out. For that person, the impact can never be the same as it is for you. The purpose of getting rid of emotional debt is to find your place in the present.

The ego has a repertoire of rationalizations for not being emotionally free:

I'm not the kind of person who feels like that.
I should be over it.
No one wants to hear about these feelings.
I don't have a right to feel hurt; it isn't fair to everyone else.
I'll only open old wounds.
The past is the past.

If you find yourself saying such things as a deflection from facing painful feelings, you may succeed in keeping them repressed. But every hidden, blocked feeling is like a chunk of frozen consciousness. Until it thaws, you are saying "I am this hurt" even as you refuse to look at it; it has you in its grip. This is another obstacle between you and the silent witness that must be dissolved. Time and attention have to be paid, sitting with your feelings and letting them say what they have to say.

Reach beyond yourself: When you are inhabiting a self that is fixed and set in place, you may think that you have attained something positive. As people say, "Now I know who I am." What they really know is an imitation of a real self, a collection of habits, labels, and preferences that is entirely historical. You have to reach beyond this self-created identity to find the source of new energy. The silent witness is not a second self. It doesn't resemble a new suit hanging in the closet that you can reach for and put on to replace the shabby suit you've worn out.

The witness is a sense of self that lies beyond boundaries. There's a haunting poem by the great Bengali poet Rabindranath Tagore in which he imagines what it will be like to die. He has a deep intuition that it will be like a stone melting in his heart:

> *The stone will melt in tears*
> *Because I can't remain closed to you forever.*
> *I can't escape without being conquered.*
>
> *From the blue sky an eye will gaze down*
> *To summon me in silence.*
> *I will receive death utterly at your feet.*

To me, this is a perfect description of reaching beyond yourself. Having lived with a hard place in the heart, you still can't avoid your real self. It is the silent eye looking down. (Instead of saying, "I will receive death," the poet could have said, "I will receive freedom" or "I will receive joy.") To reach beyond yourself means realizing, with real determination, that your fixed identity is false. Then, when the ego demands that you see the world from the perspective of "what's in it for me," you can free yourself by saying in return, "that me isn't in charge anymore."

Be genuine: Why is it said that the truth will set you free? People are punished and ostracized all the time for telling the truth. Lies often succeed. A polite agreement to go along and make no waves has brought money and power to many people. But "The truth shall set you free" wasn't meant as practical advice. There's a spiritual intent behind the words, saying in essence, "You cannot set yourself free, but truth can." In other words, truth has the power to set aside what is false, and doing so can set us free. The ego's agenda is to keep itself going. At crucial moments, however, the truth speaks to us; it tells us how things really are, not forever or for all people but right at this moment for us alone. This impulse must be honored if you wish to break free. When I think of what a flash of truth is like, some examples come to mind:

> Knowing that you can't be what someone else wants you to be, no matter how much you love the other person.
> Knowing that you love, even when it's scary to say so.
> Knowing that someone else's fight isn't yours.
> Knowing that you are better than what you appear to be.
> Knowing that you will survive.
> Knowing that you have to go your own way, no matter what the cost.

Each sentence begins with the word *knowing* because the silent witness is that level where you know yourself, without regard for what others think they know. To speak your truth isn't the same as bursting out with all the unpleasant things you've been too afraid or too polite to say. Such outbursts always have a feeling of pressure and tension behind them; they are grounded in frustration; they carry anger and hurt. The kind of truth that comes from the knower is calm; it doesn't refer to how anyone else is behaving; it brings clarity to who you are. Value these flashes. You can't make them appear, but you can encourage them by being genuine and not letting yourself fall into a persona created just to make you feel safe and accepted.

Let the center be your home: To be centered is considered desirable; when they feel distracted or scattered, people often say, "I lost my center." But if there is no person inside your head, if the ego's sense of I, me, mine is illusory, where's the center?

Paradoxically, the center is everywhere. It is the open space that has no boundaries. Instead of thinking of your center as a defined spot—the way people point to their hearts as the seat of the soul—

be at the center of experience. Experience isn't a place; it's a focus of attention. You can live there, at the still point around which everything revolves. To be off center is to lose focus, to look away from experience or block it out. To be centered is like saying "I want to find my home in creation." You relax into the rhythm of your own life, which sets the stage for meeting yourself at a deeper level. You can't summon the silent witness, but you can place yourself close to it by refusing to get lost in your own creation. When I find myself being overshadowed by anything, I can fall back on a few simple steps:

- I say to myself, "This situation may be shaking me, but I am more than any situation."
- I take a deep breath and focus my attention on whatever my body is feeling.
- I step back and see myself as another person would see me (preferably the person whom I am resisting or reacting to).
- I realize that my emotions are not reliable guides to what is permanent and real. They are momentary reactions, and most likely they are born of habit.
- If I am about to burst out with uncontrollable reactions, I walk away.

As you can see, I don't try to feel better, to be more positive, to come from love, or to change the state I'm in. We are all framed by personalities and driven by egos. Ego personalities are trained by habit and by the past; they run along like self-propelled engines. If you can observe the mechanism at work without getting wrapped up in it, you will find that you possess a second perspective, one that is always calm, alert, detached, tuned in but not overshadowed. That second place is your center. It isn't a place at all but a close encounter with the silent witness.

CHANGING YOUR REALITY TO ACCOMMODATE
THE FOURTH SECRET

This fourth secret is about meeting your real self. Words can say a great deal about the real self, but it takes an actual meeting to realize what it is. Your real self has qualities you are already experiencing every day: Intelligence, alertness, being tuned in, knowingness—whenever any of these qualities comes into play, you are living closer to your real self. On the other hand, when you feel distracted, lost, confused, fearful, scattered, or trapped inside ego boundaries, you are not.

Experience seesaws between these two poles; therefore, one way to meet your real self is to push away from the opposite pole whenever you notice that you are there. Try to catch yourself in such a moment and pull away from it. Pick a strongly negative experience of the following kind (if possible, choose a repetitive one that has cropped up several times):

- Road rage
- Arguing with your spouse
- Resenting authority at work
- Losing control over your children
- Feeling cheated in a deal or transaction
- Feeling betrayed by a close friend

Put yourself back in the situation and feel what you felt then. You might want to close your eyes and visualize the car that cut you off in traffic or the plumber who handed you the outrageous bill. Do what it takes to make the situation vivid in your mind.

When you feel that stab of anger, hurt, mistrust, suspicion, or betrayal, say to yourself, "That's how my ego feels. I can see why. I'm very used to it. I will go along as long as it lasts." Now let the feeling run. Get as worked up as your ego wants; envision fantasies of revenge or self-pity, or whatever your ego thinks is appropriate. Imagine that you are swelling up with your feeling; it spreads out from you like the shock wave from a slow-motion explosion.

Follow this wave as far as it wants to go, watching it grow fainter and fainter as it spreads to infinity, filling the whole universe if it wants to. Take deep breaths if you need to in order to get the wave of feeling to depart from you and travel outward. Don't time yourself. The feeling may be strong enough to take a while before it wants to expand.

Now, just as you see the wave disappearing into infinity, look at yourself and see if any of the following feelings are present:

- A giggle, the desire to laugh at it all
- A shrug, as if the whole thing is no big deal
- A sense of calmness or peace
- Looking at yourself as if at another person
- A deep sigh of relief or exhaustion
- A feeling of release or letting go
- A sudden realization that the other person may be right

These are the telltale feelings that arise in us when we are crossing the invisible boundary between ego and the real self. If you follow any emotion far enough, it will end in silence. But it's asking a lot to get that far every time. Your aim is to get to the frontier at least, the line where the ego's needs begin to lose their grip.

- When you laugh, you are losing the need to take yourself so seriously.
- When you shrug, you lose the need to blow things out of proportion.
- When you feel calm, you lose the need to feel agitated or to have drama.

- When you can look at yourself as if you are another person, you lose the need to be the only one who counts.
- When you feel relief or fatigue coming out, you lose the need to hold on to stress. (This is also a sign of reconnecting with your body instead of living in your head.)
- When you have the feeling of letting go, you lose the need to be vindicated—the possibility of forgiveness is in sight.
- When you suddenly realize that the other person may be right, you lose the need to judge.

There are other telltale signs of leaving ego behind. If you fall into the pattern of being easily offended, feeling either superior or inferior, wanting what is coming to you and begrudging what others get, or imagining that people are talking behind your back, each of these can be dealt with just as you did in the above instances. Relive the feeling, let your ego take it as far as it wants, and watch the feeling expand until it fades away at the edge of infinity.

This exercise won't miraculously dispel every negative feeling. Its purpose is to give you a close encounter with your real self. If you try it in that spirit, you will be surprised how much easier it becomes in the future to escape the grip of emotions that have been in control for years.

THE CAUSE OF SUFFERING IS UNREALITY

THE MOST COMMON REASON that people turn to spirituality is to deal with suffering. They don't do this by accident, but because every religion promises that it can relieve pain, that faith transcends the sorrows of the flesh, that the soul is a refuge for the suffering heart. Yet when they turn to God or faith or the soul, many people find no relief, or only the relief that otherwise might come from talking to a therapist. Is there a special power found only in spirituality? For those who turn to it, therapy works, and the most common forms of suffering, anxiety and depression, respond in the short run to drugs. When the depression lifts, is there any reason to turn to spirit?

To answer these questions we have to realize, first of all, that pain is not the same as suffering. Left to itself, the body discharges pain spontaneously, letting go of it the moment that the underlying cause is healed. Suffering is pain that we hold on to. It comes from the mind's mysterious instinct to believe that pain is good, or that it cannot be escaped, or that the person deserves it. If none of these were present, suffering would not exist. It takes force of mind to create suffering, a blend of belief and perception that the person thinks he or she has no control over. But as inescapable as suffering may appear to be, what brings escape is not attacking the suffering itself but getting at the unreality that makes us cling to pain.

The secret cause of suffering is unreality itself. Recently I saw dramatic evidence of this in a very ordinary way. I chanced on one of those television programs where people who were born with physical deformities are given a free makeover using the full powers of plastic surgery, dentistry, and the beautician's art. On this particular episode, the people who desperately wanted makeovers were identical twins. Only one twin wanted to change her looks; the other didn't. As adults, the twins no longer looked exactly alike. The "ugly one" in a given pair had suffered a broken nose or damaged teeth or had put on extra weight. The dramatic thing for me was how minor these cosmetic defects were compared to the intense belief, shared by both twins, that one was extremely beautiful and the other distressingly ugly. The "ugly ones" admitted that not a day went by without comparing themselves to their "beautiful" sisters. In this TV program one could witness all the steps that lead to suffering:

Overlooking actual facts
Adopting a negative perception
Reinforcing that perception by obsessive thinking
Getting lost in the pain without looking for a way out
Comparing yourself to others
Cementing the suffering through relationships

The handbook on how to suffer would include all these steps, which build up a sense of unreality until it seems totally real. And by implication, the directions for putting an end to suffering would reverse these steps and bring the person back to reality.

Overlooking the facts: The beginning of suffering is often a refusal to look at how the situation really is. Several years ago some researchers conducted a study to find out how people deal with crisis when it unexpectedly arises. The study was sponsored by therapists hoping to learn where people turn for help when they find themselves in trouble. When the worst misfortune occurs—when someone gets fired, has a spouse walk out, hears a diagnosis of cancer—about 15 percent seek some kind of help from a counselor, therapist, or pastor. The rest watch TV. They refuse to even consider looking at the problem or opening it up to discussion with someone who might help.

The therapists behind the study were appalled by this deep denial, but I couldn't help thinking: Isn't watching TV a natural reaction? People instinctively try to blot out pain with pleasure. Buddha faced the same situation many centuries ago. People at the time of Buddha were also trying to blot out pain because the monsoons didn't come and all their crops died, or their whole family perished in a cholera epidemic. Without TV they had to find other escapes, but the assumption was the same: Pleasure is better than pain; therefore, it must be the answer to suffering.

Replacing pleasure with pain may work in the short run. Both are sensations, and if one is strong enough it can cancel out the other. But Buddha didn't teach that life hurts because of pain; it hurts because the cause of suffering hasn't been examined. Someone can be sitting by the pool in Miami Beach, watching a favorite sitcom, eating chocolate, and being tickled with a feather at the same time. The person won't feel much pain, but she could be suffering very deeply anyway. And the only lasting way out is to take steps that will confront the source of the suffering, the first step being a willingness to look at what is actually happening.

Negative perceptions: Reality is perception, and the suffering person gets trapped by negative perceptions of his own creation.

Perception keeps the pain under control, not by reducing it but by sealing out *even greater pain.* This twist is the one most people find hard to understand. The body discharges pain automatically, yet the mind can override that instinct by turning the pain into something "good," in the sense that it's better than other, even worse possibilities. Inner confusion and conflict are why the mind has such a hard time healing itself, despite all the power it holds. The power has been turned against itself, and thus perception, which could end suffering in an instant, locks the door instead.

Reinforcing a perception: Perceptions are fluid unless we seal them in place. The self is like a constantly shifting system that incorporates the new into the old at every moment. If you constantly obsess over old perceptions, however, they become reinforced with each repetition. Let's consider a specific example. Anorexia nervosa is the medical term given to a condition in which a person, usually a girl under the age of twenty, adopts starvation as a way of life. If you interview an anorexic teenager who weighs under 90 pounds and show her four pictures of body images, ranging from the thinnest to the fattest, she will say that her body matches the fat one despite the fact that in reality her frame is skeletal. If you go so far as to superimpose her own face on the four pictures, an anorexic will still choose the fattest photo as being herself. This distorted body image totally baffles other people. It seems bizarre to look in the mirror at a skeleton and see a fat person instead (just as it is bizarre for identical twins to feel that one is extremely ugly and the other beautiful).

In these cases, perception has become distorted for hidden reasons connected to emotion and personality. An anorexic, if shown photos of four cats, can easily pick out which one is the fattest. The distortion comes at a deeper level where "I" decides what is real about oneself. The whole thing is a feedback loop. Once "I" decides something about oneself, everything in the outside world must conform to that decision. In the anorexic's mind, shame is essential to who she is, and the world has no choice but to throw her shameful image back at her. Starving herself becomes the only way she can figure out to make that fat girl in the mirror go away. Which leads to a general rule: *Reality is whatever you identify with.*

Anywhere that life hurts we have locked ourselves into some kind of false identification, telling ourselves private, unchallenged stories about who we are. The cure for anorexia is to somehow pry a wedge between "I" and this powerful, secret identification. The same applies to all suffering because each person arbitrarily identifies with one thing after another that tells an inaccurate story of who he or she is. Even if you were able to surround yourself with pleasure every minute of the day, the wrong story of who you are will wind up bringing deep suffering.

Getting lost in the pain: People have remarkably different thresholds of pain. Researchers have hooked subjects up to equal stimuli, such as electric shocks to the back of the hand, and asked them to rate the discomfort they feel on a scale from 1 to 10. It was long thought that since pain is registered along identical neural pathways, people would register a pain signal more or less the same (as for instance, almost everyone would be able to feel the difference between bright headlights in their eyes and low beams). Yet the pain that registered as a 10 for some patients felt like a 1 to others. This indicates not just that pain has a subjective component but also that the way we assess pain is completely individual. There is no universal path between stimulus and response. One person can feel deeply traumatized by an experience that hardly registers for someone else.

What's so strange about this result is that none of the subjects thought they were creating a response. If you accidentally put your hand on a hot stove, your body reacts instantly. Yet in that instant your brain is actually assessing the pain and giving it the intensity you perceive as objectively real. And by not renouncing their control over it people get lost in their pain. "What can I do? My mother just died, and I'm devastated. I can't even get out of bed in the morning." In such a statement there seems to be a direct link between cause (the death of a loved one) and effect (depression). But, in fact, the trail followed between cause and effect isn't a straight line; the whole person enters the picture, with a wealth of factors from the past. It's as if pain enters a black box before we feel it, and in that box the pain is matched up with everything we are—our whole history of emotions, memories, beliefs, and expectations. If you are self-aware, the black box isn't so sealed off and hidden. You know that you can affect what goes on inside it. But when we suffer, we victimize ourselves. Why is the pain a 10 instead of a 1? Because it just is, that's why. In truth, suffering persists only to the extent that we allow ourselves to remain lost in our own creation.

Comparing yourself to others: The ego wants to be number one; therefore, it has no choice but to get caught up in a never-ending game of comparing itself to others. Like all ingrained habits, this one is hard to break. A friend of mine recently learned that a woman he knew had been killed in a car crash. He did not know the woman well, but he knew all her friends. Within hours of her death a pall of grief had settled over them. The woman was beloved and had done many good works; she was young and full of optimism. For these reasons people grieved even more, and my friend was caught up in it. "I saw myself getting out of my car and being struck by a hit-and-run driver, the way she was. I kept thinking that I should do more than send flowers and a card. As it happened, I went on vacation the week of the funeral, and I actually found myself unable to enjoy myself just thinking about the shock and pain of dying that way."

In the midst of these reactions, my friend had a sudden realization. "I was going along getting gloomier when it hit me: 'That isn't my life. She isn't me.' The thought felt very strange. I mean, isn't it good to be compassionate? Shouldn't I share in the grief all my friends were feeling?" At that moment he stopped comparing himself to someone else—not an easy thing to do because we all gain identity from parents, friends, and spouses. An entire community has taken up fragmentary residence inside us, composed of bits and pieces of other personalities.

Our style of suffering is learned from others. To the extent that you feel stoic or weak, in control or victimized, desperate or hopeful, you are adhering to reactions set down by someone else. Deviating from their pattern feels strange, even threatening. In my friend's case, he broke out of a pattern of grief only when he realized that it was second-hand. Before that, he wanted to feel what was proper and expected. He wanted to fit in with the way others saw the situation. As long as you compare yourself to others, your suffering will persist as a way of fitting in.

Cementing suffering through relationships: Pain is a universal experience; therefore, it enters into every relationship. Nobody truly suffers alone, and even if you do everything you can to suffer in silence, you are having an effect on those around you. The reason that people find it so difficult to enter a healing relationship is that life in our family of origin often required a good deal of unawareness. We overlook what we don't want to see; we keep silent about things that are too difficult to discuss; we respect boundaries even when they put someone into a box. In short, the family is where we learn to deny pain. And denied pain is just another term for suffering.

Given a choice, most people would rather preserve their relationships than stop suffering. One sees this in abusive families where the victims don't speak up or walk out. (Some states have passed laws forcing the police to arrest domestic abusers over the protest of the spouses they beat up and torment. Without such laws, the victim sides with the abuser more than half the time.) A healing relationship is based on awareness; in it both partners work to break old habits that promote suffering. They have to walk a fine line, just as my friend did, because compassion means that you appreciate the suffering someone else is experiencing, as well as your own. Yet at the same time there has to be detachment, making sure that suffering, no matter how real, isn't the *dominant* reality. The attitudes that make for a healing relationship become part of a vision you hold for yourself and the other person.

A VISION WITHOUT SUFFERING

How to Relate When Someone Else Is in Pain

I have sympathy for you. I know what you're going through.
You don't have to feel a certain way just to make me happy.
I will help you get through this.
You don't have to be afraid that you are driving me away.
I don't expect you to be perfect. You aren't letting me down.
This pain you are going through isn't the real you.
You can have the space you need, but I won't let you be alone.
I will be as real with you as I can be.
I won't be afraid of you, even though you may be afraid of your pain.
I will do all I can to show you that life is still good and joy still possible.
I can't take your pain on as my responsibility.
I won't let you hold on to your pain—we are here to get through this.
I will take your healing as seriously as my own well-being.

As you can see, there are subtle pitfalls in these attitudes. When relating to someone in pain, you have to extend yourself and yet remain within boundaries at the same time. "I feel your pain, and yet it's not mine" is a tricky stance; it can tip either way. You can become so involved in the pain that you turn into an enabler. Or you can hide behind your own boundaries and shut out the person who is suffering. A healing relationship maintains the proper balance. You both must remain alert and attentive; you must keep your eye on the spiritual vision ahead; you must be willing to have new responses every day. Most of all, you share a path that leads, step by step, out of unreality.

The ultimate goal, if you really want to be real, is to experience existence itself. "I am" is such an experience. It is both common and rare because everyone knows how to be, yet few people extract the full promise of their own being. "I am" gets lost when you start identifying instead with "I do this, I own that, I like A but not B." These identifications become more important than the reality of your own pure being.

So let's go deeper into the link between suffering and unreality. The way we forget the peace and clarity of "I am" can be broken down into five aspects. In Sanskrit these are called the *five kleshas,* the root causes of every form of suffering.

1. Not knowing what is real
2. Grasping and clinging to the unreal
3. Being afraid of the unreal and recoiling from it
4. Identifying with an imaginary self
5. Fear of death

Right now you and I are doing one of these five things, although we began so long ago that now the process is ingrained. The five kleshas are arranged in a cascade. Once you stop knowing what is real (first klesha), the others fall into place automatically. This means that for most people only the end of the line—fear of death—is a conscious experience; therefore, we must begin there and go back up the ladder.

Being afraid of death is a source of anxiety that reaches into many areas. The way our society worships youth and shuns the elderly, our desperate need for distraction, the promotion of cosmetics and beauty treatments, flourishing gyms with full-length mirrors on all sides, and the craze for celebrity are all symptoms of wanting to deny death. Theology tries to convince us that there is life after death, but since that claim has to be taken on faith, religion exacts obedience by holding the afterlife over our heads. If we lack faith, if we worship the wrong God or sin against the right God, our chances for a reward after we die are ruined. Religious wars continue to erupt over this issue, which is so anxiety-provoking that fanatics would rather die for the faith than live with the admission that someone else's faith has a right to exist. "I die so that you may not believe in your God" is the most twisted legacy of the fifth klesha.

A person fears death not for itself but for a deeper reason, which is the need to defend an imaginary self. Identifying with an imaginary self is the fourth klesha, and it's something we all do. Even on a superficial level, people erect an image based on income and status. When Francis of Assisi, the son of a wealthy silk merchant, stripped off his rich garments and renounced his father's money, he was throwing away not just his worldly possessions but also his identity—the way people knew who he was. In his mind, God could not be approached through a false self-image.

Self-image is closely connected to self-esteem, and we know the high cost a person pays when self-esteem is lost. Children who sit in the back row in grade school and avoid the teacher's eye usually don't grow up to discuss foreign policy or medieval art because, early on, their self-image incorporated a sense of inadequacy. Conversely, studies have shown that if a teacher is told that a particular student is exceptionally bright, that student will perform much better in class even if the selection was random: Low IQ kids can achieve beyond high IQ kids with enough approval from their teachers. The image set in the teacher's mind is enough to turn a poor performer into a sterling one.

Identifying with a false image of who you are causes a great deal of suffering in other ways. Life never stops demanding more and more. The demands on our time, patience, ability, and emotions can become so overwhelming that admitting your inadequacy seems like the honest thing to do. Yet in a person's false self-image is buried the ugly history of everything that has gone wrong. "I won't," "I can't," and "I give up" all flow from the fourth klesha.

The third klesha says that even with a healthy self-image we recoil from things that threaten our egos. These threats exist everywhere. I am afraid of being poor, of losing my spouse, of breaking the law. I am afraid to shame myself before anyone whose respect I want to keep. For some people, the thought of their children turning out badly is a deep threat to their own sense of self. "We don't do that in this family" is usually code for "Your behavior threatens who I am." But people don't recognize that they are speaking in code. Once I have identified with my self-image, the fear that it might break down is instinctive. The need to protect myself from what I fear is part of who I am.

The second klesha says that a person suffers because of clinging, which means clinging to anything at all. Holding on to something is a way of showing that you are afraid it will be taken from you. People feel violated when a purse snatcher runs away with a purse, for example, or if they come home to find that the house has been broken into. These violations don't matter because of what has been taken; purses and household goods can be replaced. Yet the sense of personal injury often persists for months and years. If the right trigger is pulled, having a purse snatched can make you lose entirely your sense of personal safety. Someone has stripped you of the illusion that you were untouchable. (America's national paroxysm after the terrorist attacks on the World Trade Center continues to play out this drama of "us" versus "them" on a mass scale. The sense of American invulnerability was exposed as an illusion. Yet at bottom this wasn't a nation's problem. It was an individual problem felt on a huge scale.)

There are many twists and turns to suffering. The trail leads from fear of death to a false sense of self and the need to cling. In the end, however, unreality alone is the cause of all suffering. The problem never was pain; quite the opposite: Pain exists so that illusion won't keep getting away with its tricks. If unreality didn't hurt, it would seem real forever.

The five kleshas can be solved all at once by embracing one reality. The difference between "I am my hurt" and "I am" is small but crucial. A huge amount of suffering has resulted from this single misperception. Thinking that I was born, I cannot avoid the threat of death. Thinking that outside forces exist, I must accept that these forces can harm me. Thinking that I am a person, I see other persons everywhere. All of these are perceptions that were created, not facts. Once created, a perception lives a life of its own until you go back and change it.

It takes only a flicker of awareness to lose touch with reality. In reality nothing exists outside the self. As soon as you begin to accept this one bit of knowledge, the whole purpose of life changes. The only goal worth attaining is complete freedom to be yourself, without illusions and false beliefs.

CHANGING YOUR REALITY TO ACCOMMODATE THE FIFTH SECRET

The fifth secret is about how to stop suffering. There is a state of non-suffering inside you; it is simple and open awareness. By contrast, the state of suffering is complicated because, in its attempts to wrestle with pain, the ego refuses to see that the answer could be as simple as simply learning to be. Any steps that get you to stop clinging to complications will bring you closer to the simple state of healing. Complications occur as thoughts, feelings, beliefs, and subtle energies, meaning hidden emotional debts and resistance.

For this exercise, take anything in your life that is bringing you a sense of deep unease, discomfort, or suffering. You can choose something that has persisted for years or something that is uppermost in your life right now. Whether there is a physical component or not is unimportant, although if you pick a chronic physical disorder, don't approach this exercise as a cure—we are dealing with the patterns of perception that encourage you to hold on to suffering.

Now sit by yourself for at least 5 minutes a day for the next month with the intention of clearing away the following complications:

Disorder: Chaos is complicated, order is simple. Is your house a mess? Is your desk piled high with work? Are you letting others create messes and disorder because they know you won't make them take responsibility? Have you hoarded so much junk that your environment is like an archaeological record of your past?

Stress: Everyone feels stressed, but if you cannot completely clear your daily stress at night, returning to a calm, centered, enjoyable inner state, you are overstressed. Look closely at the things that make you tense. Is your commute stressful? Do you get up too early without enough sleep? Do you ignore signs of exhaustion? Is your body stressed by being overweight or by being totally out of shape? List the major stresses in your life and work to reduce them until you know for certain that you are not overstressed.

Empathic suffering: Getting infected with the suffering of others causes you to suffer. You have crossed the line from empathy to suffering if you feel worse after offering sympathy to someone else. If you honestly cannot be in the presence of negative situations without taking on pain that isn't yours, get away. Losing sight of your boundaries doesn't make you a "good person."

Negativity: Well-being is a simple state to which body and mind return naturally. Negativity prevents this return by causing you to dwell on not being well. Do you casually gossip about others and relish their misfortunes? Do you spend time with people who carp and criticize? Do you watch every disaster and catastrophe dished out on the evening news? These sources of negativity don't have to be engaged in—walk away and put your attention somewhere more positive.

Inertia: Inertia means giving in to old habits and conditioning. Whatever the cause of depression, anxiety, trauma, insecurity, or grief, these states linger if you take a passive attitude. "That's just how things are" is the motto of inertia. Become aware of how doing nothing is actually the way you've trained yourself to keep things the same. Do you sit and dwell on your suffering? Do you reject helpful advice before even considering it? Do you know the difference between griping and genuinely airing your feelings with the intention of healing them? Examine the routine of your suffering and break out of it.

Toxic relationships: There are only three kinds of people in your life: those who leave you alone, those who help you, and those who hurt you. People who leave you alone are dealing with your suffering as a nuisance or inconvenience—they prefer to keep their distance in order to feel better themselves. Those who help you have the strength and awareness to do more with your suffering than you are able to do by yourself. Those who hurt you want the situation to stay the same because they do not have your well-being at heart. Honestly count how many people in each category you have in your life. This isn't the same as counting friends and loving family members. Assess others solely as they relate to your difficulties.

Having made a realistic count, take the following attitude:

- I will no longer bring my problems to anyone who wants to leave me alone. It's not good for them or me. They don't want to help, so I will not ask them to.

- I will share my problems with those who want to help me. I will not reject genuine offers of assistance out of pride, insecurity, or doubt. I will ask these people to join me in my healing and make them a bigger part of my life.

- I will put a distance between myself and those who want to hurt me. I do not have to confront them, guilt-trip them, or make them the cause of my self-pity. But I cannot afford to absorb their toxic effect on me, and if that means keeping my distance, I will.

Beliefs: Examine your possible motives for wanting to suffer. Do you deny that there's anything wrong? Do you think it makes you a better person not to show others that you hurt? Do you enjoy the attention you get when you are sick or in distress? Do you feel safe being alone and not having to make tough choices? Belief systems are complex—they hold together the self we want to present to the world. It is much simpler not to have beliefs, which means being open to life as it comes your way, going with your own inner intelligence instead of with stored judgments. If you find yourself blocked by your suffering, returning to the same old thoughts again and again, a belief system has trapped you. You can escape the trap only by ending your need to cling to these beliefs.

Energy and sensations: We rely on our bodies to tell us when we are in pain, and the body, like the mind, follows familiar patterns. Hypochondriacs, for example, grasp the first sign of discomfort as a clear message that they are seriously ill. In your own case, you are also taking familiar sensations and using them to confirm your suffering. Many depressed people, for example, will interpret fatigue as depression. Because they haven't gotten a good night's sleep or have been overworked on the job, they interpret feeling depleted as a symptom of depression. The way to deal with these sensations is to strip away the interpretation. Instead of being sad, look upon this as the energy of sadness. Like fatigue, sadness has a bodily component that can be discharged. Instead of being an anxious person, deal with the energy of anxiety. All energies are discharged in the same way:

- Take a deep breath, sit quietly, and feel the sensation in your body.

- Feel the sensation without judgment. Just be with it.

- Let any feelings, thoughts, or energies that want to come up do so—this often means listening to the voice of anxiety, anger, fear, or woundedness. Let the voices say what they want to say. Listen and understand what is going on.

- Watch the energy disperse as much as it can. Don't demand complete discharge. Take the attitude that your body will let go of as much stored energy as it is able to.

- After a few hours or the next day, repeat this whole process.

This may seem like a stiff regimen, but you are being asked to spend only 5 minutes a day on any one of these areas. Tiny steps bring big results. The simple state of awareness is nature's default position; suffering and the complications that keep it going are unnatural—it wastes energy to maintain all that complexity. By working toward a simpler state every day, you are doing the best any-one can do to bring suffering to an end by cutting out the roots of unreality.

FREEDOM TAMES
THE MIND

DO YOU LOVE YOUR MIND? I've never met anyone who did. People with beautiful bodies or faces frequently love their gift from nature (although the opposite can be true—the most beautiful people physically can also shun themselves out of insecurity or fear of being seen as vain). The mind is the hardest part of ourselves to love because we feel trapped inside it—not all the time but in those moments when trouble breaks in. Fear has a way of roaming the mind at will. Depression darkens the mind; anger makes it erupt in uncontrollable turmoil.

Ancient cultures tend to echo the notion that the mind is restless and unreliable. In India, the most common metaphor compares the mind to a wild elephant, and calming the mind is said to be like tying the elephant to a stake. In Buddhism, the mind is likened to a monkey peering out at the world through the five senses. Monkeys are notoriously impulsive and fickle, liable to do anything without notice. Buddhist psychology doesn't aim to tame the monkey so much as to learn its ways, accept them, and then transcend to a higher awareness that is beyond the fickleness of the mind.

Metaphors won't get you to a place where you can love the mind; you have to find the actual experience of peace and calmness on your own. The secret for doing that is to free the mind. When it is free, the mind settles down. It gives up its restlessness and becomes a channel for peace. This is a counterintuitive solution because nobody would say that a wild elephant or a monkey can be tamed by setting it free. They'd say that the freed animal would only run wilder, yet this secret is based on actual experience: The mind is "wild" because we try to confine and control it. At a deeper level lies complete orderliness. Here, thoughts and impulses flow in harmony with what is right and best for each person.

How, then, can you set your mind free? You need to understand how it became trapped in the first place. Freedom isn't a condition you can simply step into by unlocking a door or breaking a set of shackles. The mind is its own shackle, as the poet William Blake knew when he contemplated people on the streets of London:

> *In every cry of every man*
> *In every infant's cry of fear*
> *In every voice, in every ban*
> *The mind-forged manacles I hear.*

When they tried to understand how the mind traps itself, the ancient Indian sages devised the key concept of *samskara* (from two Sanskrit word roots that mean "to flow together"). A samskara is a groove in the mind that makes thoughts flow in the same direction. Buddhist psychology makes sophisticated use of the concept by speaking of samskaras as imprints in the mind that have a life of their own. Your personal samskaras, built up from memories of the past, force you to react in the same limited way over and over, robbing you of free choice (i.e., choosing as if for the first time).

Most people build up an identity on the basis of samskara without knowing that they chose to do this. But the clues are inescapable.

Consider someone prone to attacks of rage. For these so-called rageaholics, the anger impulse is like an "it," a thing that controls them from some secret place of power. Uncontrollable outbreaks unfold in stages. First, there is usually some physical symptom—compression in the chest, the onset of a headache, rapid heartbeat, tight breathing. From there an impulse rises. The person can feel anger building up as if it were water behind a dike. The pressure is both physical and emotional; the body wants to throw off its discomfort, and the mind wants to release pent-up feelings. At this point, the person generally looks for an excuse to trigger a full-blown attack. The excuse can be found in some slight infraction—a task not performed by the children, a slow waiter, a less than courteous store clerk.

Finally, the eruption of rage occurs, and only after it settles down does the person realize the damage he has caused—the cycle ends in remorse and a promise never to erupt again. Shame and guilt enter, vowing to damp down the impulse for the future, and the mind reflects rationally on the pointlessness and risks of venting one's rage.

For any rageaholic, the element of choice is hard to reclaim. When the impulse starts to build up steam, the pressure has to find release. Often, however, there is collusion—a tacit agreement to let the rage have its way. At some time in their pasts, raging people decided to adopt anger as a coping mechanism. They saw rage at work in their family or at school. They linked power to intimidation, perhaps they had no other access to power. They typically feel unable to express themselves verbally, and striking out in anger becomes a substitute for words and thoughts. Once in the habit of raging, they stopped seeking other avenues of release. The rage they struggle to end is bound to them by need and desire—they don't know how to get what they want without it.

This is the anatomy of samskara in all its varieties. You can substitute other experiences for *rage,* such as *anxiety, depression, sexual addiction, substance abuse, obsessive compulsion;* all will testify to how samskaras rob people of free choice. Unable to escape their toxic memories, people adapt to them, adding one layer after another of impressions. The bottom layers, laid down in childhood, keep sending out their messages, which is why adults often look in the mirror and feel like impulsive, frightened children. The past has not been worked through sufficiently; samskaras rule the psyche through a jumble of old, outworn experiences.

Stored memories are like microchips programmed to keep sending out the same message over and over. When you find yourself having a fixed reaction, the message has already been sent: It does no good to try to change the message. Yet this is exactly how the vast majority of people try to tame the mind. They receive a message they don't like, and their reaction is one of three things:

Manipulation
Control
Denial

If you look at them closely, it becomes clear that all three of these behaviors come after the fact—they deal with the mind's disorder as the cause of the distress rather than as a symptom. These supposed solutions have tremendous negative effects.

Manipulation is getting what you want by ignoring or harming the desires of others. Manipulators use charm, persuasion, coaxing, trickery, and misdirection. The underlying idea is "I have to fool people to make them give me what I want." When they are really caught up in their ploys, manipulators even imagine that they are doing their victims a favor—after all, who wouldn't feel good helping out a guy who's so entertaining? You can catch yourself falling into this behavior when you aren't listening to other people, when you ignore what they want, and when you pretend that your desires cost nobody else a price. There are also external signs. The presence of a manipulator brings tension, strain, complaints, and conflict to a situation. Some people use passive manipulations—they come up with "poor me" scenarios to coax sympathy and pity out of others. Or they lay subtle guilt trips with the aim of making others think that what they want is wrong. Manipulation comes to an end when you stop assuming that your desires are all-important. Then you can reconnect with others and begin to trust that their desires might be aligned with yours. When there is no manipulation, people feel that what they want counts. They trust that you are on their side; you aren't seen as a performer or salesperson. No one feels that he or she is being fooled.

Control is forcing events and people into your way of doing things. Control is the great mask of insecurity. People who use this behavior are deathly afraid of letting others be who they are, so the controller is constantly making demands that keep others off balance. The underlying idea is "If they keep paying attention to me, they won't run away." When you find yourself making excuses for yourself and blaming others, or when you feel inside that no one is showing you enough gratitude or appreciation, the fault is not with them—you are exhibiting a need to control. The external signs of this behavior come from those you are trying to control: They are tense and resistant; they complain of not being listened to; they call you a perfectionist or a demanding boss. Control begins to end when you admit that your way isn't automatically the right way. You can tune in to your need for control by catching yourself complaining, blaming, or insisting that no one is right but you, and coming up with one excuse after another to prove that you are without blame yourself. Once you stop controlling them, the people around you begin to breathe easy. They relax and laugh. They feel free to be who they are without looking to you for approval.

Denial is looking past the problem instead of facing it. Psychologists consider denial the most childish of the three behaviors because it is so intimately linked to vulnerability. The person in denial feels helpless to solve problems, the way a young child feels. Fear is linked to denial, and so is a childlike need for love in the face of insecurity. The underlying idea is "I don't have to notice what I can't change in the first place." You can catch yourself going into denial when you experience lack of focus, forgetfulness, procrastination, refusing to confront those who hurt you, wishful thinking, false hope, and confusion. The main external sign is that others don't depend on you or turn to you when a solution is needed. By pulling your attention out of focus, denial defends with blindness. How can you be accused of failing at something you don't even see? You get past denial by facing up to painful truths. Honestly expressing how you feel is the first step. For someone in deep denial, any feeling that makes you think you are unsafe is generally one you have to face. Denial begins to end when you feel focused, alert, and ready to participate despite your fears.

Each of these behaviors tries to prove an impossibility. Manipulation tries to prove that anyone can be made to do what you want. Control tries to prove that no one can reject you unless you say so. Denial tries to prove that bad things will go away if you don't look at them. The truth is that other people can refuse to do what you want, can walk out on you for no good reason, and can cause trouble whether you face it or not. There is no predicting how long any of us will stubbornly try to prove the opposite, but only when we admit the truth does the behavior completely end.

The next thing to know about samskaras is that they are not silent. These deep impressions in the mind have a voice; we hear their repeated messages as words in our heads. Is it possible to figure out which voices are true and which are false? This is an important question because it isn't possible to think without hearing some words in your head.

Early in the nineteenth century, an obscure pastor in Denmark known as Magister Adler was fired from his church. He was con-

victed of disobeying church authorities by claiming that he had
received direct revelation from God. While preaching from the pul-
pit, he began claiming that when he spoke in a high, squeaky voice
he was speaking from revelation, whereas when he spoke with his
own normal, low voice he was speaking only as himself.

This bizarre behavior led his congregation to think their pastor
must be crazy, so they had no alternative but to fire him. As it happened, news of the case reached the great Danish philosopher Søren
Kierkegaard, who asked the really crucial question: Is it *ever* possible
to prove that someone has heard the voice of God? What behavior or
other outward sign would allow anyone to tell true revelation from
false? The disgraced clergyman would probably be diagnosed as a
paranoid schizophrenic if he showed up with the same symptoms
today. Kierkegaard concluded that Adler wasn't speaking in God's
voice, but he also observed that none of us knows where our inner
voices come from. We simply accept them, as well as the stream of
words that fill our heads.

A deeply religious person might even claim that every inner
voice is some version of the voice of God. One thing is certain, however: We all hear the inner voices of a clamoring chorus. They nag,
praise, cajole, judge, warn, suspect, disbelieve, trust, complain, hope,
love, and fear—in no special order. It's too simplistic to say that we
each have a good side and a bad side—we have thousands of aspects
formed out of past experiences. It's impossible to sort out how many
voices I am actually listening to. I sense that some are buried from
childhood; they sound like orphans of my earliest experiences begging me to take them in. Other voices are adultlike and harsh—in
them, I hear people from my past who judged or punished me. Each
voice believes that it deserves my whole attention, heedless of the
others that believe the same thing. There is no central self who rises
above the din to quell this riot of opinions, demands, and needs. At
any given moment, whatever voice I pay the most attention to

becomes *my* voice, only to be crowded offstage when my attention shifts. The unruliness that pulls me this way and that is living proof of how fragmented I have become.

How can this clamoring chorus be tamed? How can I retrieve a sense of self that fits one reality? The answer once again is freedom, yet in a most peculiar way. *You must free yourself from decisions.* The voice in your head will die down once you stop making choices. A samskara is a choice you remember from the past. Each choice changed you by a tiny fraction. The process began at birth and continues to this day. Instead of fighting it, we all believe we should keep on making choices; as a result, we keep adding new samskaras and reinforcing the old ones. (In Buddhism, this is called the *wheel of samskara* because the same old reactions keep coming around again and again. In a cosmic sense, the wheel of samskara is what drives a soul from one lifetime to the next—old imprints impel us to face the same problems time and again, even beyond death.) Kierkegaard wrote that the person who has found God has freed himself from choices. But what does it feel like to have God make your decisions for you? I think you would have to be deeply connected to God to even come close to answering that question.

Yet in a state of simple awareness, the most evolutionary choices seem to come spontaneously. While the ego agonizes over every detail of a situation, a deeper part of your awareness knows what to do already, and its choices emerge with amazing finesse and perfect timing. Hasn't everyone experienced flashes of clarity in which they suddenly know just what to do? *Choiceless awareness* is another name for free awareness. By freeing up the choice-maker inside, you reclaim your right to live without boundaries, acting on the will of God with complete trust.

Have we become trapped simply by the act of choosing? This is a surprising idea because it runs counter to a lifelong behavior. For all of us, life has been lived one choice at a time. The external world is like a huge bazaar offering a dazzling array of possibilities, and everyone shops the bazaar, cannily seizing what is best for me and mine. Most people know themselves by what came home in their shopping bag—a house, job, spouse, car, children, money. But every time you choose A over B, you are forced to leave some part of the one reality behind. You are defining yourself by selective (and completely arbitrary) preferences.

The alternative is to stop concentrating on the results and look to the cause. Who is this choice-maker inside you? This voice is a relic of the past, the accumulation of old decisions carrying over beyond their time. Right now you are living under the burden of your past self, who is no longer alive. You must protect the thousands of choices that make up this dead self. Yet the choice-maker could live a much freer life. If choices occurred in the present and were fully appreciated right now, there would be nothing left to hold on to, and then the past couldn't accumulate into a crushing burden.

Choice should be a flow. Your body already suggests that this is the natural way to exist. As we saw earlier, each cell maintains only enough reserve of food and oxygen to survive for a few seconds. Cells don't store up energy because they never know what's coming next. Flexible responses are much more important to survival than hoarding. From one viewpoint, this makes your cells look entirely vulnerable and undefended, yet as fragile as a cell may appear, two billion years of evolution can't be denied.

Everyone knows how to choose; few know how to let go. But it's only by letting go of each experience that you make room for the next. The skill of letting go can be learned; once learned, you will enjoy living much more spontaneously.

LETTING GO

How to Choose Without Getting Trapped

Make the most of every experience.
Don't obsess over right and wrong decisions.

Stop defending your self-image.

Go beyond risks.

Make no decision when in doubt.

See the possibilities in whatever happens.

Find the stream of joy.

Making the most of an experience: Living fully is extolled everywhere in popular culture. I have only to turn on the television at random to be assailed with the following messages: "It's the best a man can get." "It's like having an angel by your side." "Every move is smooth, every word is cool. I never want to lose that feeling." "You look, they smile. You win, they go home." What is being sold here? A fantasy of total sensory pleasure, social status, sexual attraction, and the self-image of a winner. As it happens, all these phrases come from the same commercial for razor blades, but living life fully is part of almost any ad campaign. What is left out, however, is the reality of what it actually means to fully experience something. Instead of looking for sensory overload that lasts forever, you'll find that the experiences need to be engaged at the level of meaning and emotion.

Meaning is essential. If this moment truly matters to you, you will experience it fully. Emotion brings in the dimension of bonding or tuning in: An experience that touches your heart makes the meaning that much more personal. Pure physical sensation, social status, sexual attraction, and feeling like a winner are generally superficial, which is why people hunger for them repeatedly. If you spend time with athletes who have won hundreds of games or with sexually active singles who have slept with hundreds of partners, you'll find out two things very quickly: (1) Numbers don't count very much. The athlete usually doesn't feel like a winner deep down; the sexual conqueror doesn't usually feel deeply attractive or worthy. (2) Each experience brings diminishing returns; the thrill of winning or going to bed becomes less and less exciting and lasts a shorter time.

To experience this moment, or any moment, fully means to engage fully. Meeting a stranger can be totally fleeting and meaningless, for example, unless you enter the individual's world by finding out at least one thing that is meaningful to his or her life and exchange at least one genuine feeling. Tuning in to others is a circular flow: You send yourself out toward people; you receive them as they respond to you. Notice how often you don't do that. You stand back and insulate yourself, sending out only the most superficial signals and receive little or nothing back.

The same circle must be present even when someone else isn't involved. Consider the way three people might observe the same sunset. The first person is obsessing over a business deal and doesn't even see the sunset, even though his eyes are registering the photons that fall on their retinas. The second person thinks, "Nice sunset. We haven't had one in a while." The third person is an artist who immediately begins a sketch of the scene. The differences among the three are that the first person sent nothing out and received nothing back; the second allowed his awareness to receive the sunset but had no awareness to give back to it—his response was rote; the third person was the only one to complete the circle: He took in the sunset and turned it into a creative response that sent his awareness back out into the world with something to give.

If you want to fully experience life, you must close the circle.

Right and wrong decisions: If you obsess over whether you are making the right decision, you are basically assuming that the universe will reward you for one thing and punish you for another. This isn't a correct assumption because the universe is flexible—it adapts to every decision you make. Right and wrong are only mental constructs. Immediately I can hear strong emotional objections to this. What about Mister Right? What about the perfect job? What about buying the best car? We are all in the habit of looking like consumers at people, jobs, and cars, wanting best value for the money. But in reality the decisions we label as right and wrong are arbitrary. Mister Right is one of a hundred or a thousand people you could spend a satisfying life with. The best job is impossible to define, given that jobs turn out to be good or bad depending on a dozen factors that come into play only after you start the job. (Who knows in advance what your co-workers will be like, what the corporate climate is, whether you will have the right idea at the right moment?) And the best car may get driven into an accident two days after you buy it.

The universe has no fixed agenda. Once you make any decision, it works around that decision. There is no right or wrong, only a series of possibilities that shift with each thought, feeling, and action that you experience. If this sounds too mystical, refer again to your body. Every significant vital sign—body temperature, heart rate, oxygen consumption, hormone level, brain activity, and so on— alters the moment you decide to do anything. A runner's metabolism can't afford to be as low as the metabolism of someone reading a book because, without increased air intake and faster heart rate, the runner would suffocate and collapse with muscle spasms.

Decisions are signals telling your body, mind, and environment to move in a certain direction. It may turn out afterward that you feel dissatisfied with the direction you've taken, but to obsess over right and wrong decisions is the same as taking no direction at all. Keep in mind that you are the choice-maker, which means that who you are is far more than any single choice you have ever made or ever will make.

Defending your self-image: Over the years you have built an idealized self-image that you defend as "me." In this image are packed all the things you want to see as true about yourself; banished from it are all the shameful, guilty, and fear-provoking aspects that would threaten your self-confidence. But the very aspects you try to push away return as the most insistent, demanding voices in your head. The act of banishment creates the chaos of your internal dia-

logue, and thus your ideal erodes even while you are doing everything to look good and feel good about yourself.

To really feel good about yourself, renounce your self-image.
Immediately you will find yourself being more open, undefended,
and relaxed. It's helpful to remember a startling comment from the
renowned Indian spiritual teacher Nisargadatta Maharaj: "If you
notice, you only have a self when you're in trouble." If that seems
unbelievable, imagine yourself walking through a dangerous neighborhood in a bad part of town. All around you are people whose
stares make you nervous; the sound of unfamiliar accents reminds
you that you are different from these people, and in that difference
you feel danger. The perception of threat causes you to withdraw by
contracting inside. This builds up a wider gap between you and what
you fear. Yet this retreat into the isolated, constricted self doesn't
really defend you from anything. It is imaginary. By widening the
gap, you only ensure that what might serve you—looking confident
and at ease—can't occur. Maharaj's point is that what we call the self
is a contraction around an empty core, whereas in reality we are
meant to be free and expansive in our awareness.

Much time is spent in self-help trying to turn a bad self-image
into a good one. As reasonable as that sounds, all self-images have
the same pitfall: They keep reminding you of who you were, not
who you are. The whole idea of I, me, and mine was erected on
memories, and these memories are not really you. If you release
yourself from your self-image, you will be free to choose *as if for the
first time.*

Self-image keeps reality away, particularly at the emotional level.
Many people don't want to admit what they are actually feeling.
Their self-image dictates that being angry, for example, or showing
anxiety is not permissible. Such feelings don't accord with the "kind
of person I want to be." Certain emotions feel too dangerous to be
part of your ideal image of yourself, so you adopt a disguise that

excludes those feelings. Deep-seated rage and fear belong in this category, but sadly so does immense joy, ecstasy, or freewheeling spontaneity. You stop being ruled by self-image when:

- You feel what you feel
- You are no longer offended by things
- You stop appraising how a situation makes you look
- You don't exclude people you feel superior or inferior to
- You quit worrying about what others think about you
- You no longer obsess over money, status, and possessions
- You no longer feel the urge to defend your opinions

Going beyond risks: As long as the future remains unpredictable, every decision involves some level of risk. That's the story that seems to be universally accepted, at least. We are told that certain foods put one at risk for heart attacks and cancer, for example, and therefore the rational thing is to quantify the risk and stay on the low side of the numbers. But life itself cannot be quantified. For every study that shows a quantifiable fact about heart disease (e.g., men who drink a quart of milk a day are half as likely to suffer a severe heart attack), there is another study to show that stress raises the risk of heart disease only if you are susceptible to stress (some people actually thrive on it).

Risk is mechanical. It implies that there is no intelligence behind the scenes, only a certain number of factors that result in a given outcome. You can go beyond risks by knowing that there is infinite intelligence at work in the hidden dimension of your life. At the level of this intelligence your choices are always supported. The point of looking at risks would be to see if your course of action is reasonable; you wouldn't rely on risk analysis to override far more important factors, the very factors that are being weighed at the level of deeper awareness:

Does this choice feel right for me?

Am I interested in where this choice is leading?

Do I like the people involved?

Is this choice good for my whole family?

Does this choice make sense given my stage in life?

Do I feel morally justified in making this choice?

Will this choice help me to grow?

Do I have a chance to be more creative and inspired by what I am about to do?

It's when these things go wrong that choices don't work out. The risks may be relevant, but they aren't decisive. People who can assess their choices at the deeper level of awareness are aligning themselves with infinite intelligence, and thus they have a greater chance for success than does someone who crunches the numbers.

When in doubt: It's hard to let go when you don't know if you have made the right choice in the first place. Doubt lingers and ties us to the past. Many relationships end in divorce because of a lack of commitment, but that lack didn't grow over time; it was present from the very outset and was never resolved. It's important not to make critical decisions when you are in doubt. The universe supports actions once they are begun, which is the same as saying that once you take a direction, you are setting a mechanism in motion that is very hard to reverse. Can a married woman feel unmarried simply because she wants to? Can you feel that you aren't your parents' child simply because you think it would be better to have different parents? In both cases the ties to a situation, once it is in place, are strong. When you are in doubt, however, you put the universe on hold for a while. It favors no particular direction.

There is a good aspect to this pause and a bad one. The good aspect is that you are giving yourself room to become aware of more things, and with more awareness, the future can bring you new reasons to act one way or the other. The bad aspect is that inertia isn't productive—without choices you cannot grow and evolve. If doubts persist, you have to break out of stasis. Most people do this by plunging into the next choice, catching life on the rebound: "This didn't work out, so I better do something else, no matter what."

Usually, the people who wind up making totally arbitrary choices—recklessly going for the next house, the next job, the next relationship that shows up—turn out to be over-calculating. They spend so much time figuring out the risks, looking at all the pros and cons, assessing every worst-case scenario, that no choice looks right, and sheer frustration pushes them to break the deadlock. Ironically, such irrational leaps sometimes work out. The universe has more in store for us than we can ever predict, and bad choices frequently smooth out in the end because our hidden aspirations know where we are going.

Even so, doubt is destructive to the one quality that awareness is trying to bring to you: knowingness. At a deep level, you are the knower of reality. Doubt is a symptom indicating that you aren't in contact with the knower inside. It usually means that you are looking outside yourself when you have to make a choice. Your decision is going to be based on externals. For most people, the strongest externals come down to what other people think because fitting in is the path of least resistance. But fitting in is like embracing inertia. Social acceptance is the lowest common denominator of the self—it's you as a social unit rather than you as a unique person. Find out who you really are; let fitting in be the last thing on your mind. Either it will happen or it won't, but in either case you will be in no more doubt about yourself.

There is no formula for removing doubts because finding the knower inside is personal. You have to be committed to expanding your awareness. Don't be in doubt about that one thing. If you turn inward and follow the path that leads to your inner intelligence, the knower will be there waiting for you.

Seeing the possibilities: It would be much easier to let go of outcomes if every choice turned out well. And why shouldn't it? In the one reality there are no wrong turns, only new turns. But the ego personality likes things to be connected. Coming in second today is better than coming in third yesterday, and tomorrow I want to come in first. This kind of linear thinking reflects a crude conception of progress. Real growth happens in many dimensions. What happens to you can affect how you think, feel, relate to others, behave in a given situation, fit into your surroundings, perceive the future, or perceive yourself. All these dimensions must evolve in order for you to evolve.

Try to see the possibilities in whatever happens. If you don't get what you expected or wished for, ask yourself, "Where am I supposed to look?" This is a very freeing attitude. On some dimension or other, every event in life can be causing only one of two things: Either it is good for you, or it is bringing up what you need to look at in order to create good for you. Evolution is win-win, which we can say not out of blind optimism but once again by referring back to the body. Anything happening inside a cell is either part of its healthy operation or a sign that a correction should take place. Energy is not expended randomly or on a whim to see how it turns out.

Life is self-correcting in just this way. As the choice-maker you can act on a whim; you can follow arbitrary or irrational paths. But the underlying machinery of consciousness doesn't alter. It keeps following the same principles, which are:

- To adapt to your desires
- To keep everything in balance
- To harmonize your individual life with the life of the cosmos
- To make you aware of what you are doing
- To show you the consequences of your action
- To make your life as real as possible

Because you have free will, you can ignore these principles entirely—we all do at one time or another. But you can't make them deviate. Life depends on them. They are the ground of existence, and even as your desires come and go, the ground of existence is unchanging. Once you absorb this truth, you can align yourself with any possibility that comes your way, trusting that win-win is the attitude that life itself has been taking for billions of years.

Finding the stream of joy: My fancy was caught by an episode in the adventures of Carlos Castaneda when his master Don Juan sends him to a witch who has the ability to adopt the perception of any creature. The witch allows Castaneda to feel exactly like an earthworm, and what does he perceive? Enormous exhilaration and power. Instead of being the tiny blind creature that a worm appears to human eyes, Castaneda felt like a bulldozer pushing each grain of dirt aside like a boulder; he was mighty and strong. Instead of feeling like drudgery, the worm's digging was cause for elation, the elation of someone who could move mountains with his body.

In your own life there is a stream of joy that is just as elemental and unshakable. A worm knows nothing but itself, so it cannot deviate from the stream of joy. You can disperse your awareness in every direction, and by doing so distract yourself from the stream. You won't really let go of your self-image and your restless mind until you feel, without question or doubt, a palpable joy in yourself. The renowned spiritual teacher J. Krishnamurti once made a passing comment I find very moving. People don't realize, he said, how important it is to wake up every morning with a song in your heart. Once I read that, I performed a test on myself. I asked inside to hear the song, and for a few weeks, without any further willpower on my part, I did notice a song as the first thing that came to mind when I woke up in the morning.

But I also know that Krishnamurti was being metaphorical: The song stands for a sense of joy in existence, a joy that is free of any good or bad choices. To ask this of yourself is both the simplest thing and the most difficult. But don't let it slip your mind, no matter how complex your life becomes. Keep before you the vision of freeing your mind, and expect that when you succeed at doing this, you will be greeted by a stream of joy.

CHANGING YOUR LIFE TO ACCOMMODATE THE SIXTH SECRET

The sixth secret is about the choiceless life. Since we all take our choices very seriously, adopting this new attitude requires a major shift. Today, you can begin with a simple exercise. Sit down for a few minutes and reassess some of the important choices you've made over the years. Take a piece of paper and make two columns labeled "Good Choice" and "Bad Choice."

Under each column, list at least five choices relating to those moments you consider the most memorable and decisive in your life so far—you'll probably start with turning points shared by most people (the serious relationship that collapsed, the job you turned down or didn't get, the decision to pick one profession or another), but be sure to include private choices that no one knows about except you (the fight you walked away from, the person you were too afraid to confront, the courageous moment when you overcame a deep fear).

Once you have your list, think of at least one good thing that came out of the bad choices and one bad thing that came out of the good choices. This is an exercise in breaking down labels, getting more in touch with how flexible reality really is. If you pay attention, you may be able to see that not one but many good things came from your bad decisions while many bad ones are tangled up in your good decisions. For example, you might have a wonderful job but wound up in a terrible relationship at work or crashed your car while commuting. You might love being a mother but know that it has drastically curtailed your personal freedom. You may be single and very happy at how much you've grown on your own, yet you have also missed the growth that comes from being married to someone you deeply love.

No single decision you ever made has led in a straight line to where you find yourself now. You peeked down some roads and took a few steps before turning back. You followed some roads that came to a dead end and others that got lost at too many intersections. Ultimately, all roads are connected to all other roads. So break out of the mindset that your life consists of good and bad choices that set your destiny on an unswerving course. Your life is the product of your awareness. Every choice follows from that, and so does every step of growth.

❁

EVERY LIFE IS SPIRITUAL

ONE OF THE PECULIARITIES of modern life is that people violently disagree over religious beliefs and then go on to lead similar lives. Nietzsche's famous remark that God is dead should be changed to God is optional. If the government kept round-the-clock surveillance on those who felt that they were abiding by divine law and those who never gave a thought about God's rule book, I imagine the sum total of virtue and vice, love and hate, peace and violence, would look exactly the same. If anything, the balance of intolerance and lovelessness would probably tilt toward the most loudly religious people in any society.

I'm not mentioning this to be contentious. Rather, it's as if the universe has a sense of humor, since at a deep level it's impossible *not* to lead a spiritual life. You and I are as deeply engaged in making a world as a saint. You can't be fired from the job of creating a world, which is the essence of spirituality. And you can't resign from the job even when you refuse to show up. The universe is living through you at this moment. With or without belief in God, the chain of events leading from silent awareness to physical reality remains intact. The operating system of the universe applies to everyone alike, and it works along principles that do not require your cooperation.

However, if you decide to lead a consciously spiritual life, a change occurs. The principles of the operating system, which means the rules of creation, become personal. We've already touched upon many of the rules of creation; let's take a look at how we can line up the universal with the personal.

UNIVERSAL

1. The universe is a mirror of consciousness.

PERSONAL

1. The events in your life reflect who you are.

Nothing in these statements smacks of religion; there isn't any spiritual vocabulary involved. Yet this first principle is the whole basis for saying that religion (whose root words in Latin mean "to tie back") unites the Creator with his creation. The physical world mirrors a mind; it carries intention and intelligence in every atom.

UNIVERSAL

2. Awareness is collective. We all draw it from a common source.

PERSONAL

2. The people in your life reflect aspects of yourself.

In this principle, we see the beginnings of all myth and archetypes, all heroes and quests. The collective psyche shares a level of awareness that goes beyond individuals. When you see other people as aspects of yourself, you are actually seeing faces of mythical types. We are one human being wearing countless masks. When all the masks are stripped off, what remains is essence, the soul, the divine spark.

UNIVERSAL

3. Awareness expands within itself.

PERSONAL

3. Whatever you pay attention to will grow.

In the one reality, consciousness creates itself, which is the same as saying that God is inside his creation. There is no place outside creation for divinity to stand—*omnipresence* means that if any place exists, God is there. But whereas God can be attentive to an infinitude of worlds, human beings use attention selectively. We put it one place and take it away from another. By paying attention we add the creative spark, and that part of our experience, either positive or negative, will grow. Violence begets violence, but so too does love beget love.

UNIVERSAL

4. Consciousness creates by design.

PERSONAL

4. Nothing is random—your life is full of signs and symbols.

The war between religion and science is old and nearly exhausted, but on one point, neither side is willing to budge. Religion sees design in nature as proof of a creator. Science sees randomness in nature as proof of no design at all. Yet, there has never been a culture based upon chaos, including the subculture of science. Consciousness looks at the universe and sees design everywhere, even if the spaces in between looked disorganized and random. For the individual, it's impossible not to see order—every aspect of life from the family outward is based on it. Your brain is set up to perceive patterns (even an inkblot looks like some kind of image, no matter how hard you try not to see one) because it took patterns of cells to make a brain. The mind is ultimately a machine for making meaning, even when it flirts with meaninglessness, as the twentieth and the twenty-first centuries have done so well.

UNIVERSAL

5. Physical laws operate efficiently, with least effort.

PERSONAL

5. At any given moment, the universe is giving you the best results possible.

Nature loves efficiency, which is very odd for something supposedly working at random. When you drop a ball, it falls straight down without taking unexpected detours. When two molecules with the potential for bonding meet, they always bond—there is no room for indecision. This expenditure of least energy, also called *the law of least effort,* covers human beings, too. Certainly our bodies cannot escape the efficiency of the chemical processes going on in each cell, so it is probable that our whole being is wrapped up in the same principle. Cause and effect aren't just linked; they are linked in the most efficient way possible. This argument also applies to personal growth— the idea is that everyone is doing the best he or she can from his or her own level of consciousness.

UNIVERSAL

6. Simple forms grow into more complex forms.

PERSONAL

6. Your inner awareness is always evolving.

This principle is baffling to the religious and scientific alike. Many religious people believe that God created the world in his image, which implies that creation had nowhere to go after that (except perhaps to devolve from its initial perfection). Scientists accept that entropy is inexorable, entropy being the tendency of energy to dissipate. Thus, in both systems it's a problem that DNA is a billion times more complex than the first primordial atoms, that the human cortex has vastly increased in size over the past 50,000 years, that life appeared out of inert chemicals, and that new thoughts appear every day out of the blue. Entropy still makes us grow old; it still causes cars to rust and stars to grow cold and die. But the drive of evolution is equally inexorable. Nature has decided to evolve, whatever our opinions about that may be.

UNIVERSAL

7. Knowledge takes in more and more of the world.

PERSONAL

7. The direction of life is from duality to unity.

According to a commonly held idea, ancient cultures saw a unified creation, while we moderns look on a fragmented and divided world. The decline of faith has been blamed for this, as has the absence of myth, traditions, and social bonding. But I believe the opposite is true: The ancient way of understanding could barely explain a sliver of all the phenomena in Nature, while physics today is on the verge of a "theory of everything." The eminent physicist John Wheeler makes a crucial point when he says that before Einstein, human beings thought that they were looking at Nature "out there," as if through a plateglass window, trying to figure out what external reality was doing. Thanks to Einstein, we realize that we are embedded in Nature; the observer changes reality by the very act of observation. Therefore, despite a widespread feeling of psychological alienation (the result of technology's outstripping our ability to keep meaning alive), the duality of man and Nature is shrinking with each successive generation.

UNIVERSAL

8. Evolution develops survival traits that perfectly match the environment.

PERSONAL

8. If you open yourself to the force of evolution, it will carry you where you want to go.

Adaptation is a miraculous thing because it proceeds by quantum leaps. When some ancestral dinosaurs developed feathers, they hit upon an adaptation that would be perfect for winged flight. The cells on the outside of their bodies, which were hard and scaly, were useful as armor, but could not contribute to soaring aloft. It's as if evolution set itself a new problem and then took a creative leap to get there. The old use of scales was abandoned for a new world of winged flight (and those same scales would take a leap in a different direction when they turned into hair, allowing the development of furry mammals). Science and religion both worry about this. Science doesn't like the notion that evolution knows where it's going; Darwinian mutations are supposed to be random. Religion doesn't like the notion that God's perfect creation changes when something new is needed. Yet this is a case where explanations have taken a backseat. Without a doubt, the physical world adapts itself by creative leaps that take place at a deeper level—call this level genetic or conscious, as you will.

UNIVERSAL

9. Chaos serves evolution.

PERSONAL

9. The fragmented mind cannot get you to unity, but you have to use it along the way.

Swirling chaos is a reality, but so is order and growth. Which is dominant? Science has yet to arrive at a conclusion because more than 90 percent of the physical universe is composed of mysterious dark matter. Since it has yet to be observed, it's an open question what the fate of the cosmos might be. Religion is firmly on the side of order, for the simple reason that God made the world out of chaos. According to science, there is a delicate balance between creation and destruction, with billions of years having elapsed in the maintenance of that balance. However, since cosmic forces on a huge scale haven't been able to rip apart the delicate fabric that wove the beginnings of life, a reasonable person might conclude that evolution is using chaos the way a painter uses the jumbled colors in his box. On the personal level, you can't reach unity while you're ruled by the whirling of thoughts and impulses in your head, but still you can use your mind to find its own source. Unity is the hidden purpose that evolution is working toward, using the fragmented mind as a tool along the way. Like the cosmos, the surface of the mind looks chaotic, but there is a tidal pool of progress at work beneath.

UNIVERSAL

10. Many invisible levels are enveloped in the physical world.

PERSONAL

10. You are living in many dimensions at once; the appearance of being trapped in time and space is an illusion.

With all their hearts, the early quantum pioneers, including Einstein, did not want to create new dimensions beyond time and space. They wanted to explain the universe as it appeared. Yet the current superstring theories that descended from Einstein use at least eleven dimensions to explain the visible world. Religion has always held that God inhabits a world beyond the five senses; science needs the same transcendent realm to explain how particles separated by billions of light years could act like mirror twins, how light can behave as both particle and wave, and how black holes can transfer matter beyond the clutches of gravity and time. Ultimately, the existence of multidimensions is irrefutable. At the simplest level, there had to be *somewhere* that space and time came from during the Big Bang, and by definition that *somewhere* can't be in time and space. Accepting that you, as a citizen of a multidimensional universe, are a multidimensional being is far from mystical, then. It's the best hypothesis one can make given the facts.

These ten principles arguably represent ways to conceive of the operating system that keeps one reality going. In truth, the whole thing is inconceivable, and our brains aren't set up to operate on inconceivable lines. They can adapt, however, to living unconsciously. Every creature on earth is subject to the laws of nature; only humans think, "What does all this matter to me?" If you opt out and decide to live as if duality is real, you won't see that these ten principles have any bearing on you. The cosmic joke is that the same laws will continue to uphold your life even though you don't recognize them.

The choice is to be conscious or not, which brings us to the possibility for transformation. No one disputes the fact that life consists of change. But can a person, simply by altering his or her consciousness, actually bring about a deep transformation and not just another superficial change? Transformation and change are two different things, as can be seen in any fairy tale. The poor girl left by her wicked stepmother to scrub the fireplace while her stepsisters go to the ball doesn't improve herself by attending night school. Cinderella is touched by a magic wand and whisked off to the palace as a completed, transformed creature.

In fairy tale logic, change is too slow, too gradual, too mundane to satisfy the yearning symbolized by the frog who knows he is a prince or the ugly duckling who becomes the beautiful swan. There's more than an element of fantasy in a magic touch that will instantaneously deliver a trouble-free life. More important, this fantasy disguises the way true transformation takes place.

The key to true transformation is that nature doesn't move forward in step-by-step movements. It takes quantum leaps all the time, and when it does, old ingredients aren't simply recombined. Something new appears in creation for the first time, an *emergent property*. For example, if you examine hydrogen and oxygen, they are light, gaseous, invisible, and dry. It took a transformation for those two elements to combine and create water, and when that happened, an entirely new set of possibilities emerged with it, the most important from our point of view being life itself.

The wetness of water is a perfect example of an emergent property. In a universe without water, wetness can't be derived by shuffling around properties that already exist. Shuffling only produces change; it isn't sufficient for transformation. Wetness had to emerge as something completely new in creation. Once you look closely enough, it turns out that every chemical bond produces an emergent property. (I gave the example in passing of sodium and chlorine— two poisons that when combined produce salt, another basic element of life.) Your body, which is bonding millions of molecules every second, depends on transformation. Breathing and digestion, to mention just two processes, harness transformation. Food and air aren't just shuffled around but, rather, undergo the exact chemical bonding needed to keep you alive. The sugar extracted from an orange travels to the brain and fuels a thought. The emergent property in this case is the newness of the thought: No molecules in the history of the universe ever combined to produce that result. Air entering your lungs combines in thousands of ways to produce cells that have never existed before in just the way they exist in you, and when you use oxygen to move, your muscles are performing actions that, however they may be similar to those of other people, are unique expressions of you.

If transformation is the norm, then spiritual transformation falls into place as an extension of where life has been going all along. While still remaining who you are, you can bring about a quantum leap in your awareness, and the sign that the leap is real will be some emergent property you never experienced in the past.

EMERGENT SPIRITUAL PROPERTIES

Clarity of awareness
Knowingness
Reverence for life
Absence of violence
Fearlessness
Nonattachment
Wholeness

These qualify as spiritual transformations because none can be achieved simply by recombining old ingredients of the self. Like the wetness of water, each appears as if by alchemy—the dross of everyday life turns to gold.

Clarity means being awake to yourself around the clock, in waking, sleeping, and dreaming. Instead of being overshadowed by externals, your awareness is always open to itself. Clarity feels totally alert, and carefree.

Knowingness means being in touch with the level of the mind where every question is answered. It is related to genius, although knowingness isn't focused on music, mathematics, or other specific subjects. Your area of knowledge is life itself and the movement of consciousness on every level. Knowingness feels wise, confident, unshakable, and yet humble.

Reverence for life means being in touch with the life force. You feel the same power flowing through you as through every living thing; even the dust in a beam of light dances to the same rhythm. Therefore, life isn't limited to plants and animals—everything possesses a glowing, animated vitality. Reverence for life feels warm, connected, and exhilarating.

Nonviolence means being in harmony with every action. There is no opposition between what you do and what anyone else does. Your desires do not clash with another person's well-being. When you look around you see conflict in the world at large but not in your world. You emanate peace like a force field that subdues conflict in your surroundings. Nonviolence feels peaceful, still, and completely without resistance.

Fearlessness means total security. Fear is a jolt from the past; it reminds us of the moment when we left a place of belonging and found ourselves in a place of vulnerability. The Bhagavad Gita says that fear is born of separation, implying that the original cause of fear was the loss of unity. Ultimately, that separation is not a fall from grace but a loss of who you really are. To be fearless feels, therefore, like yourself.

Wholeness means including everything, leaving nothing out. At present we each experience life sliced up into bits of time, bits of experience, bits of activity. We cling to our limited sense of self to protect the slices from falling apart. But it's impossible to find continuity in this way, hard as the ego tries in its struggle to make life hang together. Wholeness is a state beyond personality. It emerges when "I am" as it applies to you is the same "I am" everywhere. Wholeness feels solid, eternal, without beginning or end.

True transformation, in my view, depends on the emergence of these properties as your personal experience. They are primal qualities embedded in awareness; they weren't invented by human beings or projected out of lack, need, or hunger. You cannot experience any of them by attaining more of what you already have. Being as nice as possible to others and causing no harm isn't the same as nonviolence in the spiritual sense. Showing courage in the face of danger isn't the same as fearlessness. Feeling stable and well put together isn't the same as wholeness.

One must emphasize that however unreachable these things sound, they are completely natural—they are extensions of a process of transformation that has been with you all your life. Each of us is already an emergent property of the universe, a totally new creation from our parents' genes. And yet there is a deeper magic at work. At the chemical level, your parents' genes were only recombined; you got some from one person and some from another. The survival of a certain gene pool extended to include a new generation; it didn't suddenly break down into a new and unknown substance.

Somehow nature used those old building blocks to perform a feat of alchemy because you are not a reconfigured genetic replica. Your genes are just a supporting structure for a unique experience. DNA is the universe's way of becoming conscious of itself. It took eyes for the universe to see what it looks like, ears to hear what it sounds like, and so on. To make sure that it didn't lose interest, the universe created you so that it could be conscious of itself in a way that had never appeared before. Thus, you are an expression of eternity and of this very second, both at once.

Transforming yourself is like getting pregnant. Every woman who decides to get pregnant is making a personal decision and yet submitting to a tremendous force of nature. On the one hand, she exerts free will; on the other, she is caught up in inexorable events. Once she has a fertilized seed inside her womb, nature takes over; producing a child is something you do and at the same time it is something that is happening to you. The same can be said for any other true transformation. You can make a personal decision to be spiritual, but when spirit really takes hold, you are caught up in forces far beyond yourself. It's as if a surgeon is called into the operating room for an essential surgery and looks down to find that the patient on the table is himself.

We've covered the ten principles that serve as the operating system of one reality. But most people are firmly entrenched in another operating system—the system of duality. They live according to the assumption that they are separate, isolated individuals in a random cosmos where what happens "in here" is not reflected "out there." How, then, does a person shift from one operating system to the other? Unity is totally different from duality, but you don't have to wait for the end of this journey to live *as if* you are there in the next. Right now you are living as if limitation and separation must be true; therefore, you aren't leaving room for them *not* to be true. Even so, a hidden intelligence is preserving the incredible orderliness of life while allowing change to swirl around in apparent chaos. If exposed to sunlight on a fresh spring day, a living cell would wither and turn to dust, and its DNA would blow away in the wind. But such apparent fragility has survived two billion years of constant assault from the elements. In order to see that your own existence is protected by the same intelligence, you have to align with it first. Then a universal law reveals itself: *Wholeness remains the same no matter how much it changes.*

Your task is to make wholeness more real in your life. As long as you remain on the level where change is dominant, there is no possibility of truly becoming new. Duality maintains its operating system from moment to moment, and as long as you are plugged into it, that system seems real, workable, reliable, and self-validating. The other operating system, the one based on wholeness, works far better than the system you are used to. Wholeness is also real, workable, reliable, and self-validating. For the sake of getting our bearings, let's look at some familiar situations and see how each system would handle them.

You arrive at work one day to find out through the grapevine that your company is downsizing. No one can tell you if your job is at risk, but it might be. In the operating system of duality, the following implications start to come into play:

> I could lose the one thing I need to support myself.
> Someone else has control over my destiny.
> I am faced with something unpredictable and unknown.
> I don't deserve to be blind-sided like this.
> I could be hurt if things go wrong for me.

These are all familiar thoughts whenever you find yourself in crisis. Some people manage the threat better than others; you yourself have been through similar situations with more or less success. Yet these concerns are just part of an operating system. They are programmed into the software of the ego with its total fixation on keeping everything under control. What is really being threatened here is not the loss of a job but loss of control. This reveals just how fragile the ego's grip actually is.

Now let's reframe the situation in terms of the operating system programmed from wholeness, or one reality. You come to work to find that the company is downsizing, and the following implications begin to come into play:

> My deeper self created this situation.
> Whatever happens, there is a reason.

I am surprised, but this change doesn't affect who I am.

My life is unfolding according to what is best and most evolutionary for me.

I can't lose what's real. The externals will fall into place as they need to.

Whatever happens, I can't be hurt.

You can see immediately that plugging into the second operating system brings a far greater sense of security. Wholeness is safe; duality isn't. Protection from external threats is permanent when there are no externals but only yourself unfolding in two worlds, inner and outer, that completely mesh.

A skeptic will protest that this new operating system is only a matter of perception, and that just seeing yourself as the creator of your reality doesn't mean you are. But it does. Reality shifts as you do, and when you change your perception of being separate, the one reality responds by shifting with you. The reason everyone doesn't notice this is that the ego-based world with all its demands, pressures, drama, and excesses is highly addictive, and like any addiction it needs a daily fix as well as denial that there is any way out. By giving your allegiance to the one reality instead, you won't end the addiction immediately, but you will begin to starve it. Your ego and personality, which give you limited awareness of who you are, will be put on notice that clinging and grasping must come to an end. Your conditioning from the past that told you how to win out over the outside world will no longer help you survive. The support you counted on from external sources such as family, friends, status, possessions, and money will no longer make you feel secure.

Rest assured that perception is flexible enough to let go of the addiction to duality. Any event can be seen as coming from the creative center in oneself. At this very moment I can look at any part of my life and say "I made that." Then it is only one step away to ask "Why did I make that?" and "What do I want to make instead?"

Let's take another example: You stop at a red light on the way home, but the car behind you doesn't stop and rear-ends you. When you jump out to confront the other driver, he is not apologetic. Sullenly, he begins to give you his insurance information. In one operating system the following implications come into play:

This stranger doesn't have my best interests in mind.
If he is lying, I could be left with all the damages.
I am the aggrieved party, and he should recognize that.
I may have to force him to cooperate.

As these ideas come into play, consider the possibility that the car accident didn't cause them—they were already imprinted in your mind waiting for the moment they'd be needed. You aren't seeing the situation as it really is but only through your programmed perception. In a different operating system the following implications are equally valid:

This accident was no accident; it's a reflection of myself.
This stranger is a messenger.
When I find out why this event happened, I will uncover some aspect of myself.
I need to pay more attention to some kind of hidden or stuck energy. When I deal with it, I will be glad this accident happened.

Does the second viewpoint seem impossible, or a matter of wishful thinking? Actually, it is the natural way to perceive the situation from the viewpoint of one reality. The first viewpoint was imprinted by circumstances in your early life—you had to be trained to see others as strangers and to assume that accidents are random events. But instead of relying on such limited consciousness, you can open yourself to expanded possibilities. The larger viewpoint is more generous to you and to the other driver. You aren't antagonists but, rather, equal players in a scene that is trying to tell both of you something. The larger viewpoint holds no blame. It puts responsibility equally on every player and allows equally for growth. A car accident is neither right nor wrong—it is an opportunity to reclaim who you are, a creator. If you walk away with a result that moves you closer to your true self, you have grown, so even the ego's demand to win is satisfied by the experience of one reality.

Although you may insist that the only thing at stake here is money, and that confrontation is the best way to get paid, that view is not reality but the reinforcement of a perception. Does the money neutralize what comes with it—anger, blame, and being made a victim by others?

Wholeness brings a seamless, unified world, but you will not know what that world feels like until you give your allegiance to a new operating system. Shifting from the old system to the new one is a process, one that each of us must commit ourselves to every day. Our shared addiction to duality is total; it leaves nothing out. The good news is that no aspect of life is immune to transformation. Every change you make, however small, will be communicated throughout existence— quite literally the whole universe will be eavesdropping on you and lending you its support. From its point of view, the formation of a galaxy is no more momentous than the evolution of a single person.

CHANGING YOUR REALITY TO ACCOMMODATE THE SEVENTH SECRET

The seventh lesson is about alchemy. By any measure, alchemy is magical. You can't turn lead into gold by heating it, beating it, molding it into different shapes, or combining it with any known substance. Those are simply physical changes. Likewise, you will never cause an inner transformation by taking your old self and hammering it with criticism, heating it up with exciting experiences, reshaping how you look physically, or connecting with new people. How, then, does the magic work?

It works according to the principles that make up the universe's operating system. When you consciously align with them, you give yourself an opening for transformation. Write down the ten principles as they personally apply to you and begin to live them. Carry them around with you; refer to them as reminders every few days. It's better to focus with intention on one principle a day than trying to include too many at once. Here are examples of how you might apply these universal principles on a daily basis:

The events in my life reflect who I am: I will apply one experience today to myself. Whatever catches my attention is trying to tell me something. If I feel angry at anyone, I will see if what I dislike in the person actually exists in me. If an overheard conversation catches my attention, I will take those words as a personal message. I want to find the world that is inside me.

The people in my life reflect aspects of myself: I am a composite of every person who is important to me. I am going to look upon friends and family as a group picture of me. Each stands for a quality I want to see in myself or want to reject, yet in reality I'm the whole picture. I will gain the most knowledge from those people I intensely love and intensely dislike: The one reflects my highest aspirations; the other reflects my deepest fears of what lies inside me.

Whatever I pay attention to will grow: I will take inventory of how I'm using my attention. I will keep a log of how much time I spend with television, video games, the computer, hobbies, gossip, work I don't care about, work I am passionate about, activities that fascinate me, and fantasies of escape or fulfillment. In this way I will find out what aspects of my life are going to grow. Then I will ask, "What do I want to grow in my life?" This will tell me where my attention needs to shift.

Nothing is random—my life is full of signs and symbols: I will look for patterns in my life. These patterns could be anywhere: in what others say to me, the way they treat me, the way I react to situations. I am weaving the tapestry of my world every day, and I need to know what design I am making. I will look for signs that show me my hidden beliefs. Do I meet opportunities for success or failure? These are symbols for whether I believe I have personal power or not. I will look for signs about my belief in whether I am loved and deserve love—or not.

At any given moment, the universe is giving me the best results possible: I will concentrate today on the gifts in my life. I will focus on what is working instead of what isn't. I will appreciate this world of light and shadow. I will receive with grace the remarkable gift of awareness. I will notice how my own level of awareness makes me perceive the world I am co-creating.

My inner awareness is always evolving: Where do I stand right now? How far have I come on my chosen path? Even if I don't see immediate results outside myself, do I feel that I am growing inside? Today I will face these questions and honestly ask where I stand. I will experience my awareness not as a stream of thoughts but as the potential for becoming who I want to be. I will look at my limitations and boundaries with the intention of expanding beyond them.

The direction of life is from duality to unity: Today I want to belong. I want to feel safe and at home. I want to be aware of what it's like simply to be, without defenses or desires. I will appreciate the flow of life for what it is—my own true self. I will notice those moments of intimacy with myself, when I feel that "I am" is enough to sustain me forever. I will lie on the grass looking at the sky, feeling myself at one with nature, expanding until my being fades into the infinite.

If I open myself to the force of evolution, it will carry me where I want to go: Today is for long-term thinking about myself. What is my vision of life? How does that vision apply to me? I want my vision to unfold without struggle. Is that happening? If not, where am I putting up resistance? I will look at the beliefs that seem to hold me back the most. Am I depending on others instead of being responsible for my own evolution? Have I allowed myself to focus on external rewards as a substitute for inner growth? Today I will rededicate myself to inner awareness, knowing that it is the home of the evolutionary impulse that drives the universe.

The fragmented mind cannot get me to unity, but I have to use it along the way: What does unity really mean to me? What experiences of oneness can I look back upon? Today I will remember the difference between being at one with myself and being scattered. I will find my center, my peace, my ability to go with the flow. The thoughts and desires that drive me are not the ultimate reality. They are just a way to get myself back to oneness. I will remember that thoughts come and go like leaves in the wind, but the core of consciousness is forever. My goal is to live from that core.

I am living in many dimensions at once; the appearance of being trapped in time and space is an illusion: Today I will experience myself beyond limitations. I will set time aside to be present with myself in silence. As I breathe I will see my being spreading outward in all directions. As I settle into my own inner silence, any image that comes to mind will be asked to join my being. I will include anyone and anything that comes to mind, saying, "You and

I are one at the level of being. Come, join me beyond the drama of space and time." In the same way I will experience love as a light that begins in my heart and spreads out as far as my awareness can reach; as images arise in my mind, I will send love and light in their direction.

EVIL IS NOT YOUR ENEMY

THE MOST GRIEVOUS FAILURE of spirituality occurs in the face of evil. Idealistic and loving people who would never harm another person find themselves drawn into the maelstrom of war. Faiths that preach the existence of one God mount campaigns to kill infidels. Religions of love devolve into partisan hatred of heretics and those who threaten the faith. Even if you think you hold the ultimate truth in your hands, there is no guarantee that you will escape from evil. More violence has occurred in the name of religion than for any other reason. Hence the bitter aphorism: *God handed down the truth, and the Devil said, "Let me organize it."*

There is also the more subtle failure of passivity—standing by and letting evil have its way. Perhaps this reflects a secret belief that evil is ultimately more powerful than good. One of the most spiritual figures in the twentieth century was asked how England should handle the threat of Nazism. He replied:

> I want you to fight Nazism without arms. I would
> like you to lay down the arms you have as being use-

less for saving you or humanity. You will invite Herr
Hitler and Signor Mussolini to take what they want
of the countries you call your possessions. Let them
take possession of your beautiful island, with your
many beautiful buildings. You will give all these but
neither your souls, nor your minds.

The author of this passage was Mahatma Gandhi, and needless to say
his "open letter" to the British was greeted with shock and outrage.
Yet Gandhi was being true to the principle of *Ahimsa,* or nonviolence. He successfully used passive nonviolence to persuade the
British to grant freedom to India, so by refusing to go to war against
Hitler—a stand he took throughout World War II—Gandhi was
consistent in his spiritual beliefs. Would Ahimsa really have worked
to persuade Hitler, a man who declared that "war is the father of all
things"? We will never know. Certainly passivity itself has a dark
aspect. The Catholic Church marks as one of its darkest eras the years
when it permitted millions of Jews to be killed under Nazism, to the
extent that Italian Jews were rounded up within sight of the Vatican
windows.

So let's acknowledge that spirituality has already failed on countless occasions to deal with evil. Turning away from teachings that
have only allowed evil to propagate and spread, the one reality opens
a new way, because if there is only one reality, evil has no special
power and no separate existence. There is no cosmic Satan to rival
God, and even the war between good and evil is only an illusion born
of duality. Ultimately, both good and evil are forms that consciousness can choose to take. In that sense, evil is no different from good.
Their similarity goes back to the source. Two babies born on the same
day may grow up to commit evil on the one hand and good on the
other, but as babies it cannot be true that one was created evil. The
potential for right and wrong exists in their consciousness, and as the
babies grow up, their consciousness will be shaped by many forces.

These forces are so complex that labeling someone as purely evil makes no sense. Let me list the forces that shape every newborn child:

- Parental guidance or the lack of it
- The presence of love or its absence
- The context of the whole family
- Peer pressure at school and social pressure throughout life
- Personal tendencies and reactions
- Indoctrinated beliefs and religious teaching
- Karma
- The tide of history
- Role models
- Collective consciousness
- The appeal of myths, heroes, and ideals

Every force listed above is influencing your choices and invisibly pushing you into action. Because reality is tangled up in all these influences, so is evil. It takes all these forces for evil and good to emerge. If your childhood hero was Stalin, you won't perceive the world as you would if your hero was Joan of Arc. If you are a Protestant, your life would not have been the same under the persecution of the Huguenots as it is in an American suburb today. Think of a person as a building with hundreds of electrical lines feeding countless messages into it, powering a host of different projects. Looking at the building, you see it as one thing, a single object standing there. But its inner life depends on hundreds of signals coming into it.

So does yours.

In and of itself, none of the forces feeding into us is evil. But under this menu of influences, each person makes choices. I believe that any evil inclination comes down to a choice made in consciousness. *And those choices seemed to be good when they were made.* This is the central paradox behind evil actions, because with rare exceptions, people who perform evil can trace their motives back to decisions that were the best they could make given the situation. Children who suffer abuse, for example, frequently wind up as adults abusing their own children. You would think that they'd be the last ones to resort to family violence, having been its victim. But in their minds, other, nonviolent, options aren't available. The context of abuse, acting on their minds since early childhood, is too powerful and overshadows freedom of choice.

People in different states of awareness won't share the same definition of good and bad. A prime example is the social enslavement of women around the world, which seems totally wrong in the modern world but is fed in many countries by tradition, religious sanction, social value, and family practices, going back for centuries. Until very recently, even the victims of those forces would see the role of the helpless, obedient, childlike woman as "good."

Evil depends completely on one's level of consciousness.

You can bring this message home by considering seven different definitions of evil. Which one do you instinctively agree with?

WHAT IS THE WORST EVIL?

Seven Perspectives

1. The worst evil is to hurt someone physically, or endanger their survival.
2. The worst evil is to enslave people economically, depriving them of any chance to succeed and prosper.
3. The worst evil is to destroy peace and bring about disorder.
4. The worst evil is to entrap people's minds.
5. The worst evil is to destroy beauty, creativity, and the freedom to explore.

6. The worst evil is often difficult to tell from good, since all of creation is relative.
7. There is no evil, only the shifting patterns of consciousness in an eternal dance.

The vast majority of people would probably choose the first two definitions, because physical harm and deprivation are so threatening. At this level of consciousness, evil means not being able to survive or earn a living, and good means physical safety and economic security. In the next two levels, evil is no longer physical but mental. One's greatest terror isn't being deprived of food but rather being told what to think and forced to live with chaos and unrest. Good means inner peace and the free flow of insight and intuition. The next two levels are even more refined; they have to do with creativity and vision. One's greatest fear is not being allowed to express oneself or being forced to label others as evil. A deeply spiritual person doesn't view good and evil as rigid categories but has begun to accept that God had a purpose in creating both. Good is free expression, openness to all new things, reverence for both the dark and light aspects of life. Finally, the last level sees the entire play of good and evil, light and shadow, as an illusion. Every experience brings union with the creator; one lives as a co-creator immersed in God consciousness.

The one reality accepts all these definitions, as it must, because anything that consciousness can perceive is real to the perceiver. Evil is part of a hierarchy, a ladder of growth in which everything changes depending on the rung you happen to be standing on. Nor does the growing process ever end. It is at work in you at this very minute.

If you wake up one day to suddenly discover that you hate someone else, that there is no way out of a situation except violence, that love isn't an option, consider how subtly you arrived at your position. It took a whole world to throw you or anyone else into the arms of what is labeled as good or evil. Having internalized these forces, you reflect the world just as the world reflects you. This is what it means in practical terms to have the world in you.

Yet evil cannot be your enemy if the world is in you; it can only be another aspect of yourself. Every aspect of the self is worthy of love and compassion. Every aspect is necessary to life, and none is excluded or banished into darkness. This view may seem even more naive at first than Gandhi's passivity, for it appears that we are being asked to love and understand a murderer the same as a saint. Jesus taught exactly that doctrine. But translating love and compassion into difficult situations has been the crux of spirituality's huge failure: Violence causes love to break down, turning it into fear and hatred. *But evil doesn't actually do this.* The shaping forces on consciousness do. Here is where good and evil become equal. I can give a striking example of what I mean.

In 1971, students at Stanford University were asked to volunteer for an unusual experiment in role playing. One group of students was to pretend that they were prison guards in charge of another group who pretended to be prisoners. Although it was understood that this was make-believe, a jail setting was provided, and the two groups lived together for the duration of the experiment. According to plan, everyone would play their roles for two weeks, but after only six days the prison experiment had to be terminated. The reason? The boys chosen for their mental health and moral values turned into sadistic, out-of-control guards on the one hand and depressed victims of exorbitant stress on the other.

The professors conducting the experiment were shocked but couldn't deny what had occurred. The lead researcher, Philip Zimbardo, wrote: "My guards repeatedly stripped their prisoners naked, hooded them, chained them, denied them food or bedding privileges, put them into solitary confinement, and made them clean toilet bowls with their bare hands." Those who didn't descend to such atrocious behavior did nothing to stop the ones who did. (The parallel with infamous acts by American prison guards in Iraq in

2004 prompted Zimbardo to bring the Stanford experiment back to light after more than thirty years.) There was no extreme to which the student guards would not resort short of outright physical torture. Zimbardo mournfully recalls, "As the boredom of their job increased, they began using the prisoners as their playthings, devising ever more humiliating and degrading games for them to play. Over time, these amusements took a sexual turn, such as having the prisoners simulate sodomy on each other. Once aware of such deviant behavior, I closed down the Stanford prison."

Where did this runaway abuse come from? For comfort's sake, we usually say that it exists in a few "bad apples," but the Stanford experiment suggests something more disturbing: Evil exists in everyone as a shadow, for the very reason that the world is in everyone. Being raised as a good person is a counter to the shadow of evil, of course, and if we return to our list of shaping forces on consciousness, each person would exhibit a different map of influences. But if you are fortunate enough to have made choices on the good side of the equation, you must still acknowledge that the shadow exists in you somewhere.

The shadow was formed by the same everyday situations that shape our consciousness, and it is released by new situations that parallel them. If you were abused as a child, being around children can bring up those memories. The Stanford experimenters devised a list of conditions that cause people to do things we'd call evil, or at the very least alien to our true selves. I've expanded on it in light of what we know about dualism and separation.

INCUBATING EVIL

Conditions That Release Shadow Energies

Removing a sense of responsibility
Anonymity

Dehumanizing environments
Peer examples of bad behavior
Passive bystanders
Rigid levels of power
Prevailing chaos and disorder
Lack of meaning
Implicit permission to do harm
"Us-versus-them" mentality
Isolation
Lack of accountability

Again, are any of these conditions intrinsically evil? This list, as compared to the first, feels as if some evil component has entered. Leaving aside prisons, where one might expect the worst in human nature to emerge, as a physician I've seen similar abuse in hospital settings. Certainly, hospitals are not evil; they were established to do good in the first place. But the shadow isn't about who is good or bad. It's about sealed-up energies looking for an outlet, and a hospital is rife with the very conditions listed above: Patients are helpless under the authority of doctors and nurses; they are dehumanized by the cold mechanistic routine, isolated from everyday society, made more or less anonymous as one "case" among thousands, and so forth.

Given the right circumstances, everyone's shadow energy will emerge.

Let's focus, then, on the shadow as the area where consciousness has become distorted to the point that evil choices might be made. (Keep in mind the word "might," since even under the most dehumanized conditions, there are good people who remain good, which is to say that they are able to resist or control the release of their shadow energies.) The famed Swiss psychologist C. G. Jung was the first to use "the shadow" as a clinical term, but here I want to speak in general of the hidden places where we all repress things we feel guilty about or ashamed of. I will call this place the shadow, and I believe there are certain true things to be said about it:

> The shadow is personal and universal at the same time.
> Anything can be stored there.
> Whatever is stored in darkness becomes distorted.
> The intensity of shadow energies is a way of getting noticed.
> Bringing consciousness to any energy defuses it.
> The shadow itself is not evil and therefore not your enemy.

By examining each statement, we get closer to removing the fearful demon we label—almost always in other people—as evil incarnate.

The shadow is personal and universal at the same time: Everyone harbors a unique pattern of shame and guilt. Simple things like nudity, sexual intercourse, anger, and anxiety give rise to enormously complex feelings. In one society, seeing your mother naked could be trivial, while in another it could be such a traumatic experience that it can only be dealt with by shoving it down into the shadow. There is no sharp distinction between personal feelings, family feelings, and social feelings. They blend and weave together. But even if you feel ashamed that you hit a bully on the playground when you were seven, and another person thinks doing the same thing was a valuable moment in developing personal courage, to have a shadow is universal as well as personal. The human psyche was set up with a hiding place, and for most people that place is totally necessary, given the enormous difficulty of facing one's darkest impulses and deepest humiliations.

Anything can be stored there: A bank vault where you keep your most precious possessions is a hiding place as much as a prison dungeon. The same is true for the shadow. Although the term is used most of the time to describe a hiding place for negative energies, you have the power to turn positive to negative and vice versa. I once knew two sisters who were close as children but grew up as very different adults, the one a successful college professor, the other a twice-divorced worker at a temporary agency. The successful sister describes her childhood as wonderful; the other sister describes hers as traumatic. "Remember when Daddy locked you in the bathroom for six hours after you did something wrong?" I heard the unhappy sister say to her sibling. "That was a turning point for me. I could only imagine how angry and hopeless you felt."

The happy sister looked very surprised. "Why didn't you ask me about that? I liked being alone, so I just went inside and told myself imaginary stories. The incident was nothing." And so our stories go their separate, highly idiosyncratic ways. The same incident had no emotional charge for one sister, whereas it was a source of anger and shame for the other. Great art can be made out of scenes of violence (witness Picasso's *Guernica*) and horrors can be concocted from holy virtue (witness the crucifixion of Jesus). In the unconscious, there is a full population of unexamined impulses. The same Stanford student who might debase himself as a sadistic prison guard could also be harboring artistic talent that will never emerge unless the right situation allows the unconscious mind to release what it is holding.

Whatever is stored in darkness becomes distorted: Awareness, like fresh water, is meant to flow, and when it can't, it turns stagnant. In your inner world, there are countless memories and repressed impulses. You do not allow these to flow, which is to say to be released; therefore, they have no choice but to stagnate. Good impulses die for lack of being acted on. Love grows timid and afraid when not expressed. Hatred and anxiety loom larger than life. It is the primary property of consciousness that it can organize itself into new patterns and designs. If you don't allow consciousness to go where it needs to, however, disorganized energy is the result. For example, if you ask people to describe how they feel about their parents, a subject that most adults set aside as a thing of the past, you find that their memories from childhood are a confusing jumble. Trivial events stand out as huge traumas; other family members are simplified into cartoons; true feelings are hard or impossible to excavate. Thus, when a disturbed patient comes to a psychiatrist to be healed of a painful childhood wound, it often takes months if not years to separate fact from fantasy.

The intensity of shadow energies is a way of getting noticed: Hiding something is not the same as killing it. Shadow energies remain alive. Even though you refuse to look at them, they aren't extinguished—in fact, their desire for life becomes all the more desperate. To catch your attention as a parent, a child who is overlooked will become more and more extreme in its behavior: first a call for attention, then a cry, then a tantrum. Shadow energies follow much the same pattern. It seems only reasonable to see panic attacks, for example, as a hidden fear throwing a tantrum. That same fear first called out to be noticed in a normal way, but when the person refused to notice it, a call turned into a cry and finally ended up as a full-blown attack. Fear and anger are especially adept at increasing the voltage to the point where we feel that they are alien, evil, demonic forces acting without our will. They are actually just aspects of consciousness forced into inhuman intensity by repression. Repression says, "If I don't look at you, you will leave me alone." To which the shadow answers, "I can do things that will make you look at me."

Bringing consciousness to any energy defuses it: This follows naturally from the last statement. If an energy demands your attention, then paying attention will begin to satisfy it. An overlooked child isn't placated by one glance. It takes time to change any behavior for good or ill and, like children, our shadow energies get stuck in patterns and habits. But this doesn't alter the general truth that if you bring light into the shadow, its distortions start to lessen and eventually are healed. Is there time enough and patience to do the whole job thoroughly? There's no fixed answer to that.

Depression, for example, is a complex response that can be healed by insight, compassion, patience, caring attention from others, willingness, and professional therapy. Or you can take a pill and not bother. The choice is personal and varies from person to person. Conditions as apparently hopeless as childhood autism have been cured by parents who spent enormous amounts of time and attention to bring a child back from darkness. The darkness was a distortion in consciousness that needed light to be cured. The shadow in all its forms requires consciousness in the form of light and love, and the only limit to healing is how much of ourselves we are willing to give to the project.

The shadow itself is not evil and therefore not your enemy: If the preceding statements are true, then this one must be also. I realize that for many people there is a huge barrier in the form of "the other," someone outside themselves whose evil is unquestioned. Sixty years ago "the other" lived in Germany and Japan; thirty years ago it lived in the Soviet Union; today it lives in the Middle East. Such people find evil easier to explain by never losing sight of "the other"—without an enemy, they would have to face the presence of evil inside themselves. How much more convenient it is to know in advance that you are on the side of the angels!

Seeing the shadow in yourself defuses the whole notion of "the other" and brings closer the statement of the Roman poet Terence: *Nothing human is foreign to me.* Can absolute evil be banished so quickly, however? Polls show that a majority of people believe in the existence of Satan, and many religious sects firmly believe that the devil is loose in the world, secretly changing history through his malignant doings. It doesn't seem that good has a chance to conquer evil—perhaps their combat is eternal, never to be finally settled. But you can still choose the side you want to be on. That very fact removes the absolute from absolute evil, since by definition absolute evil would win every time, finding no obstacle in the frailty of human choice. Most people don't accept this conclusion, however. They watch the drama of good and evil as if it and not they have the power, sitting mesmerized by pictures of the latest epidemic of crime, war, and disaster.

You and I as individuals can't solve the problem of evil on a mass scale, and this sense of being powerless magnifies the belief that good in the end really isn't going to win. But to grapple with evil, you have to look at it, not in horror or as spectacle but with the same attention that you'd give to any problem you are seriously interested in. Many people find it taboo to look at evil; the theme of most horror movies is that if you come too close, you get what you deserve. But the facts about personal evil are more mundane than horrifying. In all of us, there are impulses fueled by a sense of injustice. Or we feel that someone has done us unforgivable harm from which we harbor grudges and grievances.

When you have been treated unjustly or personally harmed, the natural emotion is anger. If this anger can't get out, it festers and grows in the shadow. Lashing out when holding it back no longer works; this anger leads to a cycle of violence. Guilt can make you feel like a bad person simply for having an impulse or entertaining a thought. This is a kind of double bind: If you lash out and return the harm done to you, you have done something evil, but if you keep the anger inside and harbor it, you can feel just as evil.

Yet violence can be tamed by breaking it down into manageable bits. Negative emotions feed off certain aspects of the shadow that are very manageable:

The shadow is *dark.* Everyone has a shadow because of the natural contrast between darkness and the light.

The shadow is *secret.* We store impulses and feelings there that we wish to keep private.

The shadow is *dangerous.* Repressed feelings have the power to convince us that they can kill us or make us go insane.

The shadow is *shrouded in myth.* For generations, people have seen it as the lair of dragons and monsters.

The shadow is *irrational.* Its impulses fight against reason; they are explosive and totally willful.

The shadow is *primitive.* It's beneath the dignity of a civilized person to explore this domain, which reeks of the smell of the charnel house, the prison, the lunatic asylum, and a public lavatory.

Negativity assumes its overwhelming power from the fact that it feeds off all these qualities at once: A secret, dark, primitive, irrational, dangerous, mythical evil is much less convincing if you break it down into one quality at a time. But this process of bringing evil down to scale won't be convincing until you apply it to yourself.

So let's do that. Take a volatile issue at this moment: terrorism. By any measure, to inflict terror on innocent people is an act of cowardly, despicable evil. Now pull closer. Imagine yourself so inflamed by intolerance and religious hatred that you'd be willing to kill. (If you find that terrorism isn't charged enough for you personally, examine instead a feeling you might have based on racism, vengeance, or domestic abuse—any issue that creates a murderous impulse in you.)

No matter how evil your impulse is, it can be broken down into steps to resolve it:

Darkness: Ask yourself if it's really you having this impulse, the you whom you see in the mirror every morning.

Darkness is dealt with by bringing in the light. Freud called this replacing Id with Ego, meaning that "It" (the unnamed thing inside us) needs to be gathered back into the realm of "I" (the person you know yourself to be). In simpler terms, awareness needs to go into the place where it has been shut out.

Secrecy: Confide your evil impulse to someone you trust.

Secrecy is dealt with by honestly facing things that seem shameful or guilty. You face any and every feeling head on, without denial.

Danger: Release your anger out loud, staying with it as it decreases. Have the intention that this release is not merely venting, but truly letting go of your rage.

Danger is dealt with by defusing the bomb; that is, you find the explosive anger that lurks inside and you dispel it. Anger is the primal drive of evil impulses. Like all impulses, it comes in varying degrees, and even a towering rage can be deflated until it defuses into controlled rage, then justified anger, and on down to righteous indignation, and finally personal offense. Personal offense is not difficult to dispel, once you manage to release the built-up intensity that turns into uncontrollable rage.

Myth: Name a hero who would deal with your feelings in a different way and still remain heroic. Violence is part of heroism but so are many other positive qualities.

Myth is imaginative and creative. Therefore you can take any myth and mold it along different lines—Satan himself becomes a comic figure in medieval miracle plays, a ploy that leads directly to the comic villains in James Bond films. Myth is nothing but metamorphosis; therefore, this level gives us a powerful way to turn demons into helpers of the gods, or defeated enemies of the angels.

Irrationality: Come up with the best argument for not acting on your rage. Don't do this emotionally: See yourself as an adult counselor of a wayward teenager about to ruin his life. What would you say to make him see reason?

Irrationality is dealt with by persuasion and logic. Emotions are much more gripping and powerful than reason, but they will not be able to escape their world, where only feelings prevail, until the thinking process gives them a reason to feel differently. On their own, without mind, feelings remain the same and grow more intense over time. (A common example: Imagine yourself enraged because a kid in a red baseball cap keyed your car. He runs away and escapes. The next day you see him and run up, but when he turns around, it's a different kid. Rage turns into apology because the mind was able to introduce a simple idea: wrong person.)

Primitiveness: Without excuses or rationalizations, express your rage like a beast on a rampage—growling, howling, writhing, letting your body go. Let what's primitive be primitive, within safe bounds.

Primitive feelings are dealt with at their own level, as holdovers of the lower brain. You remove the disguise of being civilized. This level of awareness runs even deeper than emotion—the very most primitive area, known as the reptilian brain, interprets all stress as a life or death struggle for survival. At this level, your "reasonable" sense of injustice is experienced as blind panic and blind ferocity.

Even though your impulses may never cross the line into violence, ordinary impulses intensify in the shadow, where you can't see them. Whenever you hear yourself sounding resentful or angry without provocation, whenever you find yourself on the verge of tears for no reason, whenever you cannot explain why you suddenly made a rash decision, you are actually feeling the effects of energy covertly building up in the shadow.

The shadow has grown used to being repressed; therefore, to access this region of the mind doesn't happen easily. Nor is direct assault effective. The shadow knows how to resist; it can slam the door and hide its dark energy even deeper. If you recall the concept of catharsis from Greek tragedy, it was thought that only by deeply frightening the audience could they open up and feel pity. Catharsis is a form of purification. In this case it was arrived at second-hand, by having the audience see fearful actions in the life of a character on stage. But this form of trickery doesn't always work. You can go to a horror film today and come out of the theater completely unmoved, the higher brain muttering, "I've seen those special effects before." (In the same way, televised news, after fifty years of displaying gruesome images of war and violence, has done little more than inure its viewers to such images, or worse, turned them into entertainment.) Discharge is natural to the body, however, and simply by observing these shadow energies, we give them access to the conscious level of the mind.

People assume that the dark side of human nature has unstoppable power; Satan has been elevated into the equivalent of a negative God. But when it's broken down, evil turns out to be a distorted response to everyday situations. Imagine yourself sitting alone at night in an empty house. Somewhere else in the house, there's a noise. Instantly you recognize the sound of a door creaking open. Every sense goes on full alert; your body freezes. With difficulty, you resist the urge to call out, and yet a tremendous anxiety has leapt out of hiding. *A robber! A murderer!* Everyone has suffered through these agonizing seconds before the creaking door turns out to be a loose floorboard or the entry of someone coming home unexpectedly. But what really happened in that moment of dread?

Your mind took an insignificant bit of data from your environment and caused it to take on meaning. In itself, the sound of a creaking door is trivial, but if you unconsciously harbor fears of being attacked in the dark—and no one can help harboring such fears—the leap from a bit of sensory data to full-blown anxiety seems automatic. But in the gap between the noise and your reaction, an interpretation crept in, and it was the intensity of the interpretation ("Someone's breaking in! I'm going to be killed!") that created the danger.

What I'm suggesting is that evil is born in the gap between body and mind. There is no powerful ruler of the kingdom of evil. Satan started out as a moment of sensory input that got wildly out of hand. Take the fear of flying, one of the most common phobias. People who suffer from it usually have a vivid memory of when it began. They were on a flight and suddenly, just as with the creaking door, some noise of the plane or a sudden jolt made their awareness grow supersensitive. Insignificant sensations like cabin vibration and the rise and fall in the pitch of engine noise suddenly felt ominous.

Between these sensations and the reaction of fear there was a gap that lasted a fraction of a second. Tiny as it was, this gap allowed an interpretation ("We're going to crash! I'm going to die!") to attach itself to what the body was feeling. An instant later, the typical signs of anxiety—sweaty hands, dry mouth, racing pulse, dizziness, and nausea—added to the persuasiveness of the threat.

Phobics remember their first moment of uncontrollable panic without being able to take it apart in steps. Therefore, they don't see their reaction as self-induced. That fear was a by-product of the following ingredients:

Situation: A normal situation is infused with something unusual or slightly stressful.

Bodily response: We experience a physical reaction that is associated with the stress.

Interpretation: These physical signals are labeled as signs of danger, and unconsciously the mind jumps to the conclusion that the danger has to be real (the unconscious mind is very concrete, which is why nightmares seem as threatening as actual events).

Decision: The person chooses to think "I am afraid right now."

Because these ingredients fuse so quickly, they seem to be a single response, when in fact there is a chain of tiny events. Every link of the chain involves a choice. The reason we can't let raw sensation go without interpreting it is that for reasons of survival the human mind was built to find meaning everywhere. Phobias can be treated by slowly taking the phobic person back through the formative chain of events, allowing him or her to make new interpretations. By slowing the response down and giving the person time to look at it, the knot of fear can be undone. Gradually, the noises associated with flying return to their neutral, nonthreatening place.

The fleeting gap between sensation and interpretation is the birthplace of the shadow. When you go into the gap and see how intangible everything is, the ghosts begin to disperse.

Because terrorism now weighs so heavily on people's minds, the issue of mass evil cannot be avoided. The two most troubling questions are "How did ordinary people agree to participate in such evil?" and "How could innocent people become the victims of atrocities?"

The Stanford Prison Experiment and our discussion of the shadow come close to answering these questions, but I can't give one answer to satisfy all comers—any time evil is brought up, we find ourselves visited by our own shadow. *What could I have done about Auschwitz?* a voice inside us says, usually in guilty, accusing tones. No answer will ever reverse the past, but it's important to realize that no answer should be expected to.

The best approach to mass evil is not to keep remembering it but to renounce it so completely in yourself that the past is purified through you. My best answer to "How did ordinary people agree to participate in such evil?" lies in the pages you've just read. Evil is born in the gap. The gap isn't anyone's private possession. The gap contains collective responses and collective themes. When an entire society accepts the theme of "the outsiders" who cause all the trouble, then evil has everyone for a father and mother.

Yet in every case of mass evil, there were thousands of people who didn't identify with the collective impulse—they resisted, escaped, hid, and tried to save others. It's individual choice that determines whether you latch on to the collective theme and agree to play it out.

The second question, "How could innocent people become the victims of atrocities?" is more difficult, because almost everyone's mind is already closed. The questioner doesn't want a new answer. There is too much righteous anger, too much certainty that God turned his back, that no one wanted to risk their own lives to stop the enormous evil being done to others. Are you certain of these things? Being certain is the opposite of being open. When I ask myself why six million Jews perished or why equally innocent masses perished in Rwanda, Cambodia, or Stalinist Russia, my motive is first to release my own sense of anguish.

As long as I am overcome by anguish or righteous anger or horror, my ability to choose has been shut down. What I should be free to choose is purification, a return to innocence made possible by the shock of what happens when innocence isn't nurtured. You and I are responsible for our participation in the elements of evil even though we don't act out those elements on a mass scale. Believing in them keeps our participation going. So it's our duty to stop believing in "harmless" anger, jealousy, and judgment of others.

Is there some mystical reason why an innocent person becomes the target of evil? Of course not. People who talk about the karma of victims as if some hidden fate is bringing down a rain of destruction are speaking from ignorance. When an entire society engages in mass evil, outer chaos reflects inner turmoil. The shadow has erupted on a mass scale. When this happens, innocent victims are caught in the storm, not because they have some hidden karma but because the storm is so overwhelming that it engulfs everyone.

I don't view the relation of good and evil as a struggle of absolutes; the mechanism that I've been describing, in which shadow energies build up hidden power by depriving a person of free choice, is too convincing to me. I can see in myself that dark energies are at work, and being aware is the first step to illuminating the darkness. Awareness can remake any impulse. Therefore, I don't accept that evil people exist, only people who have not faced their shadows. There is always time to do that, and our souls are constantly opening new ways to bring in the light. As long as that's true, evil will never be fundamental to human nature.

CHANGING YOUR REALITY TO ACCOMMODATE
THE EIGHTH SECRET

The eighth secret is about the mind's "dark energy," to borrow a phrase from physics. The shadow exists out of sight. To find it, you have to be dedicated to a journey of descent. Think of this journey as going back to retrieve parts of your life that have been abandoned because you felt so ashamed or guilty about them. The anger that erupts from the shadow is attached to past events that were never resolved. Now those events are over and gone, but their emotional residue isn't.

Shame, guilt, and fear cannot be accessed by thinking. The shadow isn't a region of thoughts and words. Even when you have a flash of memory and recall such emotions, you are using a part of the higher brain—the cortex—that cannot touch the shadow. The journey of descent begins only when you find the doorway to the lower brain, where experience is sorted out not according to reason but according to intense feelings.

There is an ongoing drama inside your lower brain (identified with the limbic system, which processes emotions, and the reptilian brain, which reacts in terms of raw threat and survival). In this drama, many issues that would be interpreted reasonably by the higher brain—getting stuck in traffic, losing out on a business deal, being passed over at work, having a girl turn you down for a date— trigger irrational responses. Without realizing it, everyday events are causing your lower brain to draw the following conclusions:

I am in danger. I might be killed.
I must go on the attack.
I am so hurt, I will never recover.
These people deserve to die.
They put me in agony.

I don't deserve to exist.

Everything is hopeless—I'm lost in the dark forever.

I'm cursed.

Nobody loves me.

To communicate these feelings on the page, I've had to verbalize them, but in reality, the most appropriate way to view them is as energy—strong, impulsive forces that have an impetus all their own. Rest assured, no matter how free you feel from these shadow energies, they exist inside you. If they didn't, you would be in a state of total freedom, joy, and unboundedness. You would be in unity, the state of innocence regained when the hidden energy of the shadow has been purified.

Today you can begin to learn how to feel your way into the shadow. Shadow energies make themselves known whenever

You can't talk about your feelings.

You feel out of control.

You feel a flash of panic or dread.

You want to feel strongly, but your mind goes blank.

You find yourself breaking down in tears for no reason.

You have an irrational dislike for someone.

A reasonable argument turns into warfare.

You attack someone without provocation.

There are countless other ways that the shadow gets entangled in everyday situations, but these are among the most common. What they have in common is that a boundary is crossed—a controlled situation turns unexpectedly anxious or causes unexpected anger or dread. The next time you experience this, watch and see if you feel guilty or ashamed of yourself afterward; if so, then you have touched, however briefly, on the shadow.

An eruption of irrational feelings isn't the same as releasing them. Venting is not purification. So don't mistake an outburst for catharsis. Shadow energy is purified through the following steps:

- The negative feeling comes up (anger, grief, anxiety, hostility, resentment, self-pity, hopelessness).
- You ask to release it.
- You experience the feeling and follow where it wants to go.
- The feeling leaves through breath, sound, or bodily sensations.
- You have a sense of release afterward, coupled with an understanding of what the feeling meant.

It's the last step that tells the tale: When a shadow energy truly leaves, there is no resistance anymore, and you see something you didn't see before. Insight and release go together. The journey of descent consists of encountering your shadow many, many times. Emotions as intense as shame and guilt give themselves up only a bit at a time—and you wouldn't want more. Be patient with yourself, and no matter how little you think you've released, say to yourself, "That's all the energy that was willing to be let go right now."

You don't have to wait for full-blown eruptions from the shadow. Set aside a little time for a "shadow meditation," in which you give yourself permission to feel whatever wants to come up. Then you can begin the process of asking it to release.

Exercise #2: Writing as a Trigger

Another useful trigger for getting at shadow energies is automatic writing: Take a piece of paper, and start writing the sentence "I am really feeling ____ right now." Fill in the blank with any feeling that comes up—preferably a negative feeling that you had to keep to yourself that day—and keep writing. Don't stop—write as fast as you can, putting down any words that want to stream out of you.

Other sentences that you can use to begin this exercise might be:

"What I should have said was _____."
"I can't wait to tell someone that I _____."
"Nobody can stop me from saying the truth about _____."
"Nobody wants to hear me say this, but _____."

Through these triggers, you are giving yourself permission to express yourself, but the more important aim is to get at a forbidden feeling. That's why the words don't matter. Once you access the feeling, the real work of release can begin. You need to go on and feel it completely, ask for release, and keep going until you get a new bit of self-understanding. It may take practice before any real deep release comes to you, but step by step the walls of resistance will come down. The shadow is subtly involved in everyday life. It is never so hidden that you cannot bring it to light.

Secret #9

❁

YOU LIVE IN
MULTIDIMENSIONS

LAST WEEK I MET TWO PEOPLE who could start a spiritual feud if they weren't so gentle. The first was a woman with a conscience. Having realized a fortune in the clothing business, she knew that much of the finery we put on our backs is made under sickening conditions in the Third World, where children work sixteen-hour days for pennies. Having seen these conditions firsthand, the woman became a dedicated activist.

"We have to wipe out slave labor," she told me with passion in her voice. "I can't understand why everyone isn't outraged by what's going on." I could tell that she really wanted to know why *I* wasn't outraged. Her eyes, with the intense, feverish gaze, were fixed on me. "You of all people," they said. Not that I needed reminding. When you live a life publicly associated with spirituality, people want to know why their brand of spirituality isn't the one you embrace. In this case, the woman with a conscience thought that the highest form of spirituality was humanitarianism; to her way of thinking you aren't really spiritual unless you help the poor and fight injustice and inequality.

A few days later, I met her opposite in a man who earns his living performing healing at a distance. He was born in South America and found out, through mysterious experiences as a child, that he could see into the subtle world of auras and energy fields. For a long time nothing came of this gift; he was in the import-export business until he was over forty. Then one day he fell ill and found himself going to a healer who cured him without laying on hands—simply by moving his energy psychically. From that moment on, the man became passionate about doing the same kind of work. And he, too, wanted to know why I wasn't following his version of spirituality.

"Changes are about to happen on the astral plane," he said in a low, reserved tone. "Science has been in power on the material plane, but there's going to be a turnaround in 2012—I've been told this by my spirit guides. From that year on, science will decline, destroyed by its own excesses. Then spirit will return to the planet."

Instead of a passionate humanitarianism, this man advocated detachment and withdrawing from the material world. Like the first woman, he couldn't understand why I didn't catch on—it was obvious to him that trying to change the world by confronting it was hopeless.

Strangely enough, I agreed with both of them. What they represented was a secret: Each of us lives in multidimensions. We can choose where to focus our attention, and wherever that focus goes, a new reality opens up. Even though they disagreed with each other, both of these people were trying to solve the same problem, which is how to be spiritual despite the demands of materialism. And the answers they found are both viable, without either one being *the* answer.

When I speak of other dimensions, I'm referring to domains of consciousness. Consciousness is the maker of reality—we've been talking about that for some time here—but *maker* really means "chooser." The one reality already possesses every possible dimension;

no one needs to make new ones, or could if they wanted to. But through our attention we bring these dimensions to life: We populate them, add new meaning, and paint unique pictures. Let me name these domains first.

THE INVISIBLE DOMAINS

How Awareness Unfolds from the Source

Pure being: The domain of the Absolute, pure awareness before it acquires any qualities at all. The state before creation. This is not actually a separate domain since it permeates everything.

Conditioned bliss: The domain of awareness as it begins to become conscious of its own potential.

Love: The motivating force in creation.

Knowingness: The domain of inner intelligence.

Myth and archetypes: The collective patterns of society. This is the domain of gods and goddesses, heroes and heroines, male and female energy.

Intuition: The domain where the mind understands the subtle mechanics of life.

Imagination: The domain of creative invention.

Reason: The domain of logic, science, and mathematics.

Emotion: The domain of feelings.

Physical body: The domain of sensation and the five senses.

Which of these realms is truly spiritual? They all interconnect, yet you can observe quite often that people camp out in one realm or another, and having found their special place, they also find spirit there.

The woman with a conscience found her place in emotions and the physical body—it was the physical struggle of day-to-day poverty that moved her heart. But, of course, one can't exclude love from her set of motives; perhaps she also intuitively knew that this kind of humanitarian work was the path of greatest growth for herself.

The man who healed from a distance found his place in the realm of intuition. This is where the subtle energies play. His brand of spirituality called for manipulating the invisible forces that hold the physical world together. One can't exclude love from his set of motives, and there's also the realm of myth and archetype to be considered since he called on angels and spirit guides to do his work.

A skeptic might argue that these realms simply don't exist. That's a hard argument to settle because if something doesn't exist *for you,* it might as well not exist. This might be the moment to look at a simple example.

A car is found run into a snowbank after a winter storm. The driver is unconscious at the wheel. People stop to see what's wrong, and they ask each other, "How did this happen?" One points to the tire tracks in the snow: "The car veered off course—that's how this happened." Another observer points to the steering wheel, which is wrenched to one side: "The car's steering mechanism was faulty— that's how this happened." A third observer smells the driver's breath: "He was drunk—that's how this happened." Finally, a neurologist happens to stop by with a portable MRI machine, and he points to the driver's brain scan: "His motor cortex exhibits abnormalities—that's how this happened."

Every answer depends entirely upon the kind of evidence used. The same question was asked at different levels of reality, and at each level only one kind of answer made sense. The neurologist isn't the enemy of the car mechanic; he just thinks that his own answer is deeper and therefore more true.

When people argue that there is no scientific proof that the universe is conscious, my immediate response is, "I am conscious, and am I not an activity of the universe?" The brain, which operates on electromagnetic impulses, is as much an activity of the universe as are the electromagnetic storms in the atmosphere or on a distant star. Therefore, science is one form of electromagnetism that spends its time studying another form. I like the remark that a physicist once made to me: "Science should never be considered the enemy of spirituality because science is its greatest ally. Science is God explaining God through a human nervous system. Isn't spirituality the same thing?"

A philosopher might argue that reality isn't truly known until you include all layers of interpretation. In that sense, the theory of one reality doesn't fight against materialism—it expands it. The driver who ran into the snowbank could have had many levels of motivation: Maybe he was depressed and drove off the road on purpose (emotions). Maybe he was thinking about a poem he wanted to write and his attention wandered (imagination). Maybe he saw in his mind's eye that an oncoming car was about to swerve into his lane (intuition).

To get to a new level of explanation, you have to transcend the level you are on, to go beyond it. If you can acknowledge that going beyond is something you do every day, there is no great reason to use materialism as a club to beat spirituality over the head. The material world can be your base level of experience or not. The other levels are available by transcending, or going beyond your base level, as you are doing this second when your brain turns chemistry into thoughts.

So the real question is what domain you wish to live in. To me, the ideal life is lived on all levels of consciousness. Your attention is not bounded or narrow; you open yourself to the whole of awareness. You have an opportunity to lead such a life, but by focusing on one or two levels only, you've caused the others to atrophy. They have been squeezed out of your awareness, and thus your ability to transcend is much diminished. (On the most mundane level it's often a matter of finding the time. I rarely meet scientists who have given consciousness a second thought—they are too wrapped up in lab work. Like the rest of us, their plates are full, and if the world could have a profoundly different basis from what they learned as a pre-med or in quantum physics, the typical scientist will look into it tomorrow.)

Each dimension of your existence has its own purpose, offering a level of fulfillment that is not available anywhere else (these are the "flavors of creation"). In completely expanded awareness, every dimension is accessible.

WHEN THE DOORS ARE OPEN

Living in All Dimensions of Awareness

Pure being: When this door is open, you know yourself as the "I am," the simple state of eternal existence.

Conditioned bliss: When this door is open, you feel liveliness and vibrancy in the midst of all activity. Bliss is beyond pleasure and pain.

Love: The domain of bliss as a personal experience. When this door is open, you experience love in every aspect of life. Love is your primary motivation in every relationship, beginning with yourself. At a deeper level, love bonds you to the rhythm of the universe.

Knowingness: This is the source of the mind. When this door is open, you can access wisdom and knowledge about anything in creation.

Myth and archetypes: When this door is open, you shape your life as a quest. You reach for the same attainments as your revered heroes and heroines. You also play out the eternal dynamic between masculine and feminine.

Intuition: When this door is open, you can shape these subtle forces for healing, clairvoyance, and insight into human nature.

Intuition also guides you on your own path, showing you how to decide which path to travel as your life changes course.

Imagination: When this door is open, the images in your mind have creative power. They breathe existence into possibilities that never existed before. At this level, you also develop a passion for exploring the unknown.

Reason: When this door is open, you can make up systems and models for reality. Rational thought copes with infinite possibilities by using logic, which cuts off slices of reality to analyze in isolation from the whole.

Emotion: When this door is open, you are sensitive to bodily sensations and interpret them as pleasure and pain, feelings you desire and those you want to avoid. The emotional domain is so powerful that it overrides logic and reason.

Physical body: When this door is open, you find yourself as a separate being in the physical world.

How did all these levels come about? As a fact of existence: Pure being conceived them, projected them from itself, and then entered them. This is the cosmic circuit board, and your own nervous system is wired into it. By paying attention to any dimension of life, you send a current of consciousness into it. If you pay no attention, the circuit is closed for that dimension. Although we are using words like *doors, circuitry,* and *levels,* they fall short of reality, which vibrates with every impulse. You are having an effect in every dimension, even when you haven't sent your attention to explore and understand what's there.

Someone who has fully explored a dimension is said in Sanskrit to have attained *Vidya,* a word that literally means "knowledge" but implies much more—mastery over a set of natural laws. Think of yourself as entering a workshop where the tools and skills are unknown to you. The minute you step inside you take in everything at a glance, but it requires training to master every detail. In the end you emerge as a changed person, with completely altered perceptions. Thus, a musician coming out of the Juilliard School of Music hears every note on the radio through a different nervous system from someone who has just graduated from M.I.T. as an electrical engineer. Both have acquired Vidya, the kind of knowledge that you become rather than the kind you passively learn.

People with vastly different visions of spirituality still have in common a quest for Vidya. They want to be transformed by knowledge that flows directly from the source—the fact that one person's source is God while another's is Brahman, Allah, Nirvana, or Being is a minor difference. What really divides people is keeping the doors of perception shut. This state is called *Avidya,* or lack of awareness.

AVIDYA

Cutting Yourself Off from Awareness

Pure being: When this door is closed, we exist in separation. There is underlying dread of death, a loss of connection, and the absence of any divine presence.

Conditioned bliss: When this door is closed, life is joyless. Happiness is only a passing state. There is no opening for peak experiences.

Love: When this door is closed, life is heartless. We feel isolated in a gray world where other people are distant, detached figures. There is no sense of a loving hand in creation.

Knowingness: When this door is closed, the laws of nature are baffling. Knowledge is gained only through facts and limited personal experience, with no access to deeper meaning.

Myth and archetypes: When this door is closed, there are no higher models, no heroes or gods, no passionate quests to pursue. We see no mythical significance to our own lives. There is no deeper dimension to the relations between men and women beyond what lies on the surface.

Intuition: When this door is closed, life loses its subtlety. The person lacks insight, has no flashes of brilliance, no exhilarated "Aha!" moments. The subtle web of connectedness that holds the universe together is completely hidden from view.

Imagination: When this door is closed, the mind is devoid of fantasy. We see everything in literal terms—art and metaphor count very little. Important decisions are approached with technical analysis, and there is no hope of a sudden creative leap.

Reason: When this door is closed, life makes no sense. We are ruled by random impulses. No course of action can be followed to its conclusion, and decisions are made irrationally.

Emotion: When this door is closed, feelings are frozen. There is little or no room for compassion and empathy. Events seem disconnected, without flow, and other people present no chance for bonding.

Physical body: When this door is closed, life is all mental. The person feels that his or her body is inert, a dead weight to drag around. The body exists as a necessary life support system, nothing more. There is no "juice" to moving and acting in the world.

As you can see, there is no single state of Avidya but many. Traditionally in India, the distinction wasn't so subtle and people were typed as either being in ignorance or being enlightened. Unless you were in unity, so the thinking went, you were in utter ignorance. (The rough equivalent in the West would be that you were either lost or redeemed.) Thus, the number of those in Vidya was minuscule, while the numbers in Avidya were enormous.

But tradition overlooked the mechanics of awareness. We are multidimensional creatures, and therefore a person can attain Vidya in one area but not another. Picasso was a superb artist (imagination) but a terrible husband (love); Mozart a divine creator of music (imagination and love) but weak physically; Lincoln a master of myth and archetype but devastated emotionally. In your own life these same imbalances occur. As long as we are working to move from Avidya to Vidya, we are leading a spiritual life.

CHANGING YOUR REALITY TO ACCOMMODATE THE NINTH SECRET

The reason Christ, Buddha, Socrates, or any other spiritual teacher speaks to us personally is that limited consciousness does give way to sudden, clear glimpses of a reality beyond. Your mind *wants* to transcend. Narrow attention is like a single light that shines on only one object. It excludes everything outside its beam; the equivalent in the mind is rejection. But what if you renounced the entire process of rejection? If you did so, you would find yourself paying attention to everything equally. Rejection is a habit. Without it, you can participate in life as it comes to you.

Take each domain of awareness and write down how you keep yourself from entering it. In this way you become aware of what you are doing to limit your consciousness, and by catching yourself in time, each of these ingrained reflexes can begin to change. For example:

Pure being: I don't slow down enough to be truly quiet inside. I don't set time aside to meditate. I haven't experienced the tranquillity in nature recently. Now I will catch myself rejecting inner peace and find time for it.

Conditioned bliss: I haven't felt joy in simply being alive. I am not seeking opportunities for wonder. I don't seem to be around young children enough. I haven't gazed at the night sky. Now I will catch myself rejecting joyful appreciation and make time for it.

Love: I've been taking my loved ones for granted, so I haven't been expressing my love very much. I feel uncomfortable receiving love from others. I've put love on the back burner as something I value. Now I will catch myself rejecting these opportunities to make love important in my life and make time for it.

Knowingness: I give in to doubt too much. I automatically take a skeptical stance and only settle for hard facts. I don't seem to know any wise people, and I spend little time exposing myself to philosophy and spiritual writings. Now I will catch myself rejecting traditional wisdom and make time for it.

Myth and archetypes: I don't really have any heroes anymore. I can't remember finding a worthy example in anything or anyone for a long time. I go my own way, which is as good as anyone else's. Now I will catch myself rejecting the notion that a higher inspiration is necessary and find time for it.

Intuition: I use my head. I don't go for anything as mushy as intuition. I look for proof before I believe in something. I think all extrasensory powers are wishful thinking. I analyze a given situation and make my decision accordingly. Now I will catch myself rejecting my first hunches and start trusting them.

Imagination: Art's not my thing. I don't go to museums or concerts. My hobby is television and the sports page. To me, most creative types don't have their feet on the ground. Now I will catch myself rejecting my imagination and find ways to express it.

Reason: I know what I know and stick with it. I don't listen to the other side of an argument very often—I just want to prove I'm right. I tend to have the same reactions to similar situations. I don't always follow through with the plans I make, even when they're good. Now I will catch myself being unreasonable and will stop to consider every point of view.

Emotion: I don't make a scene and I hate it when anyone else does. I'm not impressed by people who give in to their emotions.

Holding it inside is my motto—nobody ever sees me cry. I can't remember anyone growing up who taught me that emotions are positive. Now I will catch myself rejecting my real feelings and find a safe way to express them.

Physical body: I should take care of myself. I'm in considerably worse shape physically than I was five or ten years ago. I'm not happy with my body, and I'm not much for physical activity. I've heard about body therapies, but I think they're indulgent and a little flaky. Now I will catch myself giving up on the physical side of my life and make time for it.

Of necessity, I've provided very general notes, but you should be as specific as possible. Under "Love," write down the name of someone you haven't shown your love to or an incident you recall where you felt uncomfortable receiving love. Under "Imagination," note the museum in town you don't visit or the artistic person whose company you've avoided. By the same token, be specific if you can about how you are going to change these habits of rejection.

Exercise #2: My Awareness Profile

Now that you've taken notice of where your limitations lie, draw up a profile of your awareness as it is today. Keep the profile in a safe place and consult it sixty days from now to see how much you've changed. The profile is rated in each category from 1 to 10. When you return after the sixty days are up, rate yourself without first looking at your original scores.

0 pts.	I don't pay any attention to this part of my life.
1–3 pts.	I have had a little experience in this area but not recently and not very often.
4–6 pts.	I am familiar with this area of my life and experience it fairly often.

7–9 pts.   This is an important area of my life, one that I focus on a lot.

10 pts.   This area is my home. I know it well and spend almost all my extra attention on it.

(0–10 pts.)

_____	*Pure Being*
_____	*Conditioned Bliss*
_____	*Love*
_____	*Knowingness*
_____	*Myth and Archetypes*
_____	*Intuition*
_____	*Imagination*
_____	*Reason*
_____	*Emotion*
_____	*Physical Body*

Secret #10

DEATH MAKES LIFE
POSSIBLE

I IMAGINE THAT IF SPIRITUALITY sought sales advice from
Madison Avenue, it would be, "Scare people about dying." This tactic has been working for thousands of years. Because all we can see of
death is that once you die you aren't here anymore, this creates deep
fear. There has never been a time when people weren't desperate to
know what lies "on the other side of life."

But what if there is no "other side"? Perhaps death is only relative, not a total change. After all, each of us is dying every day, and
the moment known as death is really just an extension of this
process. St. Paul spoke of dying unto death, by which he meant having such strong faith in the afterlife and the salvation promised by
Christ that death lost its power to generate fear. Yet dying unto
death is also a natural process that has been going on in cells for billions of years. Life is intimately entwined with death, as you can
observe every time a skin cell is sloughed off. This process of exfoliation is the same as a tree dropping its leaves (the Latin word for
"leaf" is *folio*), and biologists tend to think of death as a means for
life to regenerate.

This view brings little comfort, however, when you face being the leaf falling off the tree to make room for next spring's growth. Rather than discussing death in impersonal terms, I'd like to focus on *your* death, the supposed end of the you who is alive at this moment and wants to remain so. The personal prospect of death is the issue no one likes to confront, yet if I can show you what the reality of your death is, all this aversion and fear can be conquered, after which you can pay more attention to both life and death.

Only by facing death can you develop real passion for being alive. Passion isn't frantic; it isn't driven by fear. Yet right now, at an unconscious level, most people feel they are snatching life from the jaws of death, frantic with the knowledge that their time on earth is so brief. When you see yourself as part of eternity, however, this fearful snatching of crumbs from the table vanishes, and in its place you receive the abundance of life that we hear so much talk about but that so few people seem to possess.

Here's a simple question: When you are a grandparent, you will no longer be a baby, a teenager, or a young adult. So when it comes time to go to heaven, which of these people is going to show up? Most people look totally baffled when they're asked this question. It's not a frivolous one. The person you are today isn't the same person you were when you were ten years old. Certainly your body has changed completely from that of the ten-year-old. None of the molecules in your cells is the same, and neither is your mind. You certainly don't think like a child.

In essence, the ten-year-old you once were is dead. From a ten-year-old's perspective, the two-year-old you once were is also dead. The reason that life seems continuous is that you have memories and desires that tie you to the past, but these too are ever shifting. Just as your body comes and goes, so does the mind with its fleeting thoughts and emotions. When you are aware of being yourself without being attached to any particular age, you've found the mysterious observer within who doesn't come and go.

Only witnessing awareness qualifies as that observer—it remains the same while everything else changes. The witness or observer of experience is the self to whom all experiences are happening. It would be futile to hold on to who you are at this moment in terms of body and mind. (People are baffled by which self they are going to take to heaven because either they imagine an ideal self going there or a self they have attached to their imaginations. At some level we all know that there was never an age that felt ideal, however.) Life needs to be fresh. It needs to renew itself. If you could beat death and remain just who you are—or who you were at the time of life you consider the best—you'd succeed only in mummifying yourself.

You are dying at every moment so that you can keep creating yourself.

We have already established that you are not in the world; the world is in you. This, the main tenet of the one reality, also means that you are not in your body; your body is in you. You are not in your mind; your mind is in you. There is no place in the brain where a person can be found. Your brain consumes not one molecule of glucose to maintain your sense of self, despite the millions of synaptic bursts that sustain all the things that self is doing in the world.

So when we say that the soul leaves a person's body at the moment of death, it would be more correct to say that the body leaves the soul. The body is already coming and going; now it leaves without coming back. The soul can't leave because it has nowhere to go. This radical proposition needs a bit of discussion because, if you aren't going anywhere when you die, you must be there already. This is one of those paradoxes from quantum physics whose understanding depends upon knowing where things come from in the first place.

Sometimes I ask people a simple question such as, "What did you eat for dinner last night?" When they say "chicken salad" or "steak," I then ask, "Where was that memory before I asked you?" As we've already seen, there's no picture of a chicken salad or a steak imprinted in your brain—nor any taste or smell of food. When you bring a memory to mind, you are actualizing an event. Synaptic firings produce the memory, replete with visuals, taste, and smell if you want them. Before you actualize it, a memory is not local, meaning it has no location; it is part of a field of potential, or energy, or intelligence. That is, you have the potential for memory, which is infinitely vaster than a single memory but nowhere in sight. This field extends invisibly in all directions; the hidden dimensions we've been discussing can all be explained as different fields embedded in one infinite field, which is being itself.

You are the field.

We all make a mistake when we identify with the events that come and go in the field. These are isolated moments—single blips as the field momentarily gets actualized. The underlying reality is pure potential, which is also called the soul. I know how abstract this sounds, and so did the ancient sages of India. Looking at creation, which is filled with objects of the senses, they came up with a special term, Akasha, to fit the soul. The word *Akasha* literally means "space," but the larger concept is of soul space, the field of awareness. When you die, you don't go anywhere because you are already in the dimension of Akasha, which is everywhere. (In quantum physics, the tiniest subatomic particle is everywhere in spacetime before it gets localized as a particle. Its nonlocal existence is just as real but invisible.)

Imagine a house with four walls and a roof. If the house burns down, the walls and roof collapse. But the space inside isn't affected. You can hire an architect to design a new house, and after you build it, the space inside still hasn't been affected. By building a house you are only dividing unbounded space into inside and outside. This division is an illusion. The ancient sages said that your body is like that house. It's built at birth and burns down when you die, yet the Akasha, or soul space, remains unchanged; it remains unbounded.

According to these ancient sages, the cause of all suffering, according to the first klesha, is not knowing who you are. If you are the unbounded field, then death is not at all what we've feared.

The purpose of death is to imagine yourself into a new form with a new location in space and time.

In other words, you imagine yourself into this particular lifetime, and after death you will dip back into the unknown to imagine your next form. I don't consider this a mystical conclusion (in part because I've had discussions with physicists who support this possibility, given all they know about the nonlocality of energy and particles), but it's not my intention to convert you to a belief in reincarnation. We're just following one reality to its hidden source. Right now you are bringing up new thoughts by actualizing your potential; it seems only reasonable that the same process produced who you are now.

I own a TV set with a remote control, and when I push a button I can change from CNN to MTV to PBS. Until I press the remote, those programs don't exist on the screen; it's as if they don't exist at all. Yet I know that each program, complete and intact, is in the air as electromagnetic vibrations waiting to be selected. In the same way, you exist in Akasha before your body and mind pick up the signal and express it in the three-dimensional world. Your soul is like the multiple channels available on TV; your karma (or actions) picks the program. Without believing in either one, you still can appreciate the astonishing transition from a potential hanging around in space—as TV programs do—to a full-blown event in the three-dimensional world.

What, then, will it be like when you die? It might be like changing channels. Imagination will continue to do what it has always been doing—popping new images up on the screen. Some traditions believe that there's a complex process of reliving karma when you die so that a person can learn what this lifetime was about and prepare to make a new soul bargain for the next lifetime. The moment of death is described as having your life flash before you, not at lightning speed as experienced by people when they're drowning, but slowly and with full understanding of every choice one has made since birth.

If you are conditioned to think in terms of heaven and hell, going to one or the other will be your experience. (Remember that the Christian conception of these places isn't the same as the Islamic version or the thousands of *Lokas* in Tibetan Buddhism, which makes room for a multitude of worlds after death.) The creative machinery of consciousness will produce the experience of that other place, while to someone who has led the same life under no such belief system, these images might appear to be a blissful dream or a reliving of collective fantasies (like a fairy tale), or the unspooling of themes from childhood.

But if you go to another world after death, that world will be in you as much as this one is. Does that mean heaven and hell are not real? Look out the window at a tree. It has no reality except as a specific spacetime event being actualized out of the infinite potential of the field. Therefore, it's only fair to say that heaven and hell are just as real as that tree—and just as unreal.

The absolute break between life and death is an illusion.

What bothers people about losing the body is that it seems like a terrible break or interruption. This interruption is imagined as going into the void; it is total personal extinction. Yet that perspective, which arouses huge fears, is limited to the ego. The ego craves continuity; it wants today to feel like an extension of yesterday. Without that thread to cling to, the journey day to day would feel disconnected, or so the ego fears. But how traumatized are you by having a new image come to mind, or a new desire? You dip into the field of infinite possibilities for any new thought, returning with a specific image out of the trillions that could possibly exist. At that moment, you aren't the person you were a second ago. So, you are clinging to an illusion of continuity. Give it up this moment and you will fulfill St. Paul's dictum to die unto death. You will realize that you have been discontinuous all along, constantly changing, constantly dipping into the ocean of possibilities to bring forth anything new.

Death can be viewed as a total illusion because you are dead already. When you think of who you are in terms of I, me, and mine, you are referring to your past, a time that is dead and gone. Its memories are relics of a time passed by. The ego keeps itself intact by repeating what it already knows. Yet life is actually unknown, as it has to be if you are ever to conceive of new thoughts, desires, and experiences. By choosing to repeat the past, you are keeping life from renewing itself.

Do you remember the first time you tasted ice cream? If not, look at a very young child encountering an ice cream cone. The look on the child's face tells you that she is lost in pure delight. But the second ice cream cone, although a child may beg and plead for it, is slightly less wonderful than the first. Each repetition pales by degrees because, when you return to what you already know, it can't be experienced for the first time. Today, as much as you may like ice cream, the experience of eating it has become a habit. The sensation of taste hasn't changed, but you have. The bargain you made with your ego, to keep I, me, and mine going on the same habitual tracks, was a bad bargain—you have chosen the opposite of life, which is death.

Technically speaking, even the tree outside your window is an image from the past. The instant you see it and process it in your brain, the tree has already moved on at the quantum level, flowing with the vibrating fabric of the universe. To be fully alive you have to inject yourself into the nonlocal domain where new experiences are born. If you drop the pretense of being in the world, you will realize that you've always lived from the discontinuous, nonlocal place called the soul. When you die you will enter the same unknown, and in that moment you will have a good chance of feeling that you were never more alive.

Why wait? You can be as alive as you want to be through a process known as surrender. This is the next step in conquering death. So far in this chapter the line between life and death has become so blurry that it has almost disappeared. Surrender is the act of erasing the line entirely. When you can see yourself as the total cycle of death within life and life within death, you have surrendered—the mystic's most powerful tool against materialism. At the threshold of the one reality, the mystic gives up all need for boundaries and plunges directly into existence. The circle closes, and the mystic experiences himself as the one reality.

SURRENDER IS . . .

Full attention
Appreciation of life's richness
Opening yourself to what is in front of you
Nonjudgment
Absence of ego
Humility
Being receptive to all possibilities
Allowing love

Most people think of surrender as a difficult, if not impossible, act. It connotes surrender to God, which few except the most saintly seem to manage. How can one tell that the act of surrender has happened? "I am doing this for God" sounds inspiring, but a video camera in the corner of the room couldn't tell the difference between an act performed for God and the same act performed without God in mind.

It's much easier to do the surrendering on your own and let God show up if he wants to. Open yourself up to a Rembrandt or Monet painting, which is after all as glorious a piece of creation as there is. Pay full attention to it. Appreciate the depth of the image and the care in its execution. Open yourself up to what is in front of you rather than allowing yourself to be distracted. Don't judge in advance that you have to like the painting because you've been told it's great. Don't force yourself to respond because it makes you look smart or sensitive. Let the painting be the center of your focus, which is the essence of humility. Be receptive to any reaction you may have. If all these steps of surrender are present, then a great Rembrandt or Monet will evoke love because the artist is simply *there* in all his naked humanity.

In the presence of such humanity, surrender isn't difficult. People themselves are more difficult. Yet surrendering to someone else follows the same steps we just listed. Perhaps the next time you sit down to dinner with your family you might decide to concentrate on just one step of surrender, such as paying full attention or being non-judgmental.

Pick the step that seems easiest to approach or, better yet, the one that you know you've been leaving out. Most of us have left out humility when we relate to our families. What does it mean to be humble with a child, for example? It means regarding the child's opinion as equal to your own. At the level of awareness, it *is* equal; your advantage of years as the parent at the table doesn't discount that fact. We all had to be children, and what we thought back then had all the weight and importance of life at any age, perhaps more so. The secret of surrender is that you do it inside, without trying to please anyone else.

As much as it disturbs us, eventually we all find ourselves in the presence of someone who is very old, frail, and dying. The same steps of surrender are possible in that situation. If you follow them, the beauty of a dying person is just as evident as the beauty of a Rembrandt. Death inspires a certain wonder that can be reached when you go beyond the knee-jerk reaction of fear. I recently felt this sense of wonder when I came across a phenomenon in biology that helps support the whole notion that death is completely wedded to life. It turns out that our bodies have found the key to surrender already.

The phenomenon is called *apoptosis*. This strange word, which was completely new to me, takes one on a deeply mystical journey; and having returned, I find my perceptions of life and death have changed. Punching *apoptosis* into an Internet search engine gave me 357,000 entries, and the very first defined the word in biblical terms: "For every cell there is a time to live and a time to die."

Apoptosis is programmed cell death, and although we don't realize it, each of us has been dying every day, right on schedule, in order to remain alive. Cells die because they want to. The cell carefully reverses the birth process: It shrinks, it destroys its basic proteins, and then it goes on to dismantle its own DNA. Bubbles appear on the surface membrane as the cell opens its portals to the outside world and expels every vital chemical, to finally be swallowed up by the body's white cells exactly as they would devour an invading microbe. When the process is complete, the cell has dissolved and leaves no trace behind.

When you read this graphic account of a cell sacrificing itself so methodically, you can't help being touched. Yet the mystical part is still to come. Apoptosis isn't a way to get rid of sick or old cells, as you might suppose. The process gave us birth. As embryos in the womb, each of us passed through primitive stages of development when we had tadpole tails, fishlike gills, webbing between our fingers, and most surprisingly, too many brain cells. Apoptosis took care of these unwanted vestiges—in the case of the brain, a newborn baby forms proper neural connections by removing the excess brain tissue that we were all born with. (It came as a surprise when neurologists discovered that our brains contain the most cells at birth, a number which gets whittled down by the millions so that higher intelligence can forge its delicate web of connections. It was long thought that killing off brain cells was a pathological process associated with aging. Now the whole issue must be reconsidered.)

Apoptosis doesn't end in the womb, however. Our bodies continue to thrive on death. The immune cells that engulf and consume invading bacteria would turn on the body's own tissues if they didn't induce death in each other and then turn on themselves with the same poisons used against invaders. Whenever any cell detects that its DNA is damaged or defective, it knows that the body will suffer if this defect is passed on. Fortunately, every cell carries a poison gene known as p53 that can be activated to make itself die.

These few facts barely scratch the surface. Anatomists long ago knew that skin cells die every few days; that retinal cells, red blood cells, and stomach cells also are programmed with specific short life spans so that their tissues can be quickly replenished. Each dies for its own unique reason. Skin cells have to be sloughed off so that our skin remains supple, while stomach cells die as part of the potent chemical combustion that digests food.

Death cannot be our enemy if we have depended upon it from the womb. Consider the following irony. As it turns out, the body is capable of taking a vacation from death by producing cells that decide to live forever. These cells don't trigger p53 when they detect defects in their own DNA. And by refusing to issue their own death warrants, these cells divide relentlessly and invasively. Cancer, the most feared of diseases, is the body's vacation from death, while programmed death is its ticket to life. This is the paradox of life and death confronted head on. The mystical notion of dying every day turns out to be the body's most concrete fact.

What this means is that we are exquisitely sensitive to the balance of positive and negative forces, and when the balance is tipped, death is the natural response. Nietzsche once remarked that humans are the only creatures who must be encouraged to stay alive. He couldn't have known that this is literally true. Cells receive positive signals that tell them to stay alive—chemicals called growth factors. If these positive signals are withdrawn, the cell loses its will to live. Like the Mafia's kiss of death, the cell can also be sent messengers that bind to its outer receptors to signal that death has arrived— these chemical messengers are actually known as "death activators."

Months after writing this paragraph I met a Harvard Medical School professor who had discovered an amazing fact. There is a substance that causes cancer cells to activate new blood vessels so that they can get food. Medical research has focused on finding out how to block this unknown substance so that malignant growths can be deprived of nutrients and thus killed. The professor discovered that the exact *opposite* substance causes toxemia in pregnant women, a potentially fatal disorder in which the blood vessels are "unhappy" that they are undergoing normal programmed cell death. "You realize what this means?" he said with deep awe. "The body can trigger chemicals in a balancing act between life and death, and yet science has totally ignored who is doing the balancing. Doesn't the whole secret of health lie in that part of ourselves, not in the chemicals being used?" The fact that consciousness could be the missing ingredient, the X factor behind the scenes, came to him as a revelation.

The mystics have preempted science here because one reads in many mystical traditions that every person dies at exactly the right time and knows in advance when that time is. But I would like to examine more deeply the concept of dying every day. To die every day is a choice everyone overlooks. I want to see myself as the same person from day to day in order to preserve my sense of identity. I want to see myself as inhabiting the same body every day because it is disturbing to think that my body is constantly deserting me.

Yet it must, if I am not to be a living mummy. Following the complex timetable of apoptosis, I am given a new body via the mechanism of death. This process happens subtly enough that it passes without notice. No one sees a two-year-old turning in her body for a new one at age three. Every day she has the same body, and yet she doesn't. Only the constant process of renewal—a gift of death—enables her to keep pace with each stage of development. The wonder is that one feels like the same person in the midst of such endless shape-shifting.

Unlike with cell death, I can observe my ideas being born and dying. To support the passage from childish thought to adult thought, the mind has to die every day. My cherished ideas die and never reappear; my most intense experiences are consumed by their own passions; my answer to the question "Who am I?" totally changes from age two to three, three to four, and so on throughout life.

We understand death when we drop the illusion that life must be continuous. All of nature obeys one rhythm—the universe is dying at the speed of light yet it still manages along the way to create this planet and the life forms inhabiting it. Our bodies are dying at many different speeds at once, beginning with the photon, ascending through chemical dissolution, cell death, tissue regeneration, and finally the death of the whole organism. What are we so afraid of?

Apoptosis rescues us from fear, I think. The death of a single cell makes no difference to the body. What counts is not the act but the plan—an overarching design that brings the balance of positive and negative signals that every cell responds to. The plan is beyond time because it dates to the very construction of time. The plan is beyond space because it is everywhere in the body and yet nowhere—every cell as it dies takes the plan with it, and yet the plan survives.

In the one reality, you don't settle an argument by picking sides—both sides of any argument are equally true. So I have no trouble conceding that what happens after death is invisible to the eye and cannot be proved as a material event. I concede without question that we normally don't remember our past lives and can live very well without that knowledge. Still, I don't understand how anyone can remain a materialist after seeing apoptosis at work. The case against life after death looks strong only if you ignore everything discovered about cells, photons, molecules, thoughts, and the whole body. Every level of existence is born and dies on its own timetable, from less than a millionth of a second to the probable rebirth of a new universe billions of years from now. The hope that lies beyond death comes from the promise of renewal. If you passionately identify with life itself instead of with the passing parade of forms and phenomena, death takes its rightful place as the agent of renewal. In one of his poems, Tagore asks himself, "What will you give / When death knocks at your door?" His answer displays the untroubled joy of someone who has risen above the fear surrounding death:

> *The fullness of my life—*
> *The sweet wine of autumn days and summer nights,*
> *My little hoard gleaned through the years,*
> *And hours rich with living.*

> *That will be my gift*
> *When death knocks at my door.*

CHANGING YOUR REALITY TO ACCOMMODATE THE TENTH SECRET

The tenth secret says that life and death are naturally compatible. You can make this secret personal by shedding the image of yourself that belongs to the past—a kind of exfoliation of your self-image. The exercise is very simple: Sit with your eyes closed and see yourself as an infant. Use the best baby picture you can remember, or if you don't recall such an image, create one.

Make sure the baby is awake and alert. Catch its attention and ask it to look into your eyes. When you've made contact, just gaze for a moment until you both feel settled and connected to each other.

Now invite the baby to join you and slowly watch the image fade into the center of your chest. You can visualize a field of light that absorbs the image if you want, or just a warm feeling in your heart.

Now see yourself as a toddler. Again, make contact and once you have, ask that version of you to join you. Proceed in this way through any past self you wish to bring to mind—if you have particularly vivid memories of a certain age, linger there, but ultimately you want to see every image fade and disappear.

Continue up to your present age, and then go on to see yourself in stages older than you are now. End up with two final images: one of you as a very old person but in good health, and one of you on your deathbed. In each case make contact, and then let the image be absorbed into you.

When the image of yourself dying is gone, sit quietly and feel what remains. No one can actually imagine his or her own death because, even if you go to the extent—which may be too gruesome for many people—of seeing yourself as a corpse being lowered into the grave and decomposing to its elements, the witness will remain. Visualizing yourself as a corpse is an ancient Tantric exercise from India, and I have led groups through it. Almost everyone gets the point, which has nothing to do with gruesomeness: When you see every earthly vestige of yourself vanish, you realize you will never succeed in extinguishing yourself. The presence of the witness, who is the ultimate survivor, points the way beyond the dance of life and death.

Exercise #2: Dying Consciously

Like every experience, dying is something you create as much as something that is happening to you. In many Eastern cultures, there is a practice called "conscious death," in which the person participates actively in shaping the dying process. Using prayer, rituals, meditation, and assistance from the living, the dying person shifts the balance from "this experience is happening to me" to "I am creating this experience."

In the West, we don't have a tradition of conscious death. In fact, we leave dying people alone in impersonal hospitals where the routine is cold, frightening, and dehumanizing. There is much to change on that front. What you can do personally at this moment is to bring your awareness to the dying process, ridding it of excessive fear and anxiety.

Think of someone close to you who is elderly and close to dying. See yourself in the room with the person—you can imagine the room if you don't have actual knowledge of where the person is. Put yourself inside the mind and body of the person. See yourself in detail; feel the bed, see the light coming in through the window, and surround yourself with the faces of family and attending doctors and nurses, if there are any.

Now begin to assist the person in the shift from passively facing death to actively creating the experience. Hear yourself talking in a normal voice; there's no need for solemnity. Be comforting and reassuring, but focus primarily on shifting the person's awareness from "this is happening to me" to "I am doing this." Here are the main themes to talk about (I've put them in the second person, as if confiding in a close friend):

I think you've had a beautiful life. Let's talk about the best things you remember.

You can be proud of having turned out to be a good person.

You have created a lot of love and respect.

Where would you like to go from here?

Tell me how you feel about what's happening. How would you change it if you could?

If you have any regrets, tell me about them. I'll help you let go of them.

You have no more need for sorrow. I'll help you let go of any that you still feel.

You deserve to be at peace. You have run your race well, and now that it's finished, I'll help you home.

You won't believe this, but I envy you. You are about to see what's behind the curtain.

Is there anything you want for your journey?

You can, of course, bring the same themes to the bedside of someone who is truly dying. But having an imaginary conversation is a good way to reach down into yourself. The process shouldn't be a once-over-lightly. Each topic could last an hour. To be really engaged, you'll need to feel that you are giving yourself ample attention. This exercise should bring up very mixed feelings, since we all harbor fear and sorrow at the prospect of death. If you have someone in your life who died before you were able to bid them a complete farewell, imagine talking to the person about the themes I just listed. The domain where life and death merge is always here with us, and by paying attention to it you connect yourself to a precious aspect of awareness. Dying in full awareness is completely natural if you have lived in full awareness.

❁

THE UNIVERSE THINKS
THROUGH YOU

I RECENTLY HAD A SMALL ENCOUNTER with destiny—so small that I could have ignored it entirely. A man came to visit me who had devoted his entire life to spirituality. He told me about his many visits to India and his devotion to its ways. He wore amulets of the kind you can buy at temples and holy sites; he knew many sacred chants, or Bhajans; he had been blessed by many holy men in his travels. Some had given him mantras as a gift. A mantra can be as short as a syllable or as long as a sentence, but it's basically a sound. In what way can a sound be a gift? To someone steeped in the Indian tradition, the gift isn't the mantra itself but the effect it's meant to bring, such as wealth or a good marriage. There are thousands of mantras and thousands of possible results they bring.

When I asked him what he did for a living, the man waved his hand and said, "Oh, a little healing, a little psychic stuff. You know, mind-reading. I don't pay much attention to it."

His careless attitude intrigued me, and I asked if he could show me an example. He shrugged. "Think of somebody and write down a question you want to ask them." The only person on my mind that day was my wife, who had been visiting family in New Delhi for a while. I reminded myself that I should call to ask her when she was planning to return—we hadn't set a fixed date since some of the family members were elderly, and my wife's stay depended on how well they were doing.

I wrote this down and looked at my visitor. He closed his eyes and began to chant a long mantra. After a minute he said, "Tuesday. You're thinking about your wife, and you want to know when she's coming home."

He had got it right, and after he left and I was able to phone my wife, he got the day of her return right, too. I congratulated him, but he smiled and waved his hand with the same careless gesture that said, "It's nothing. I barely pay attention to it." An hour later, when I was alone, I began to think about these psychic events, which are no longer a novelty, given how the media play up paranormal phenomena. Specifically, I wondered about free will and determinism. This man said he could read minds, but my wife's return on Tuesday wasn't on my mind. It was an event that could have fallen on any day of the week; I had even supposed that she might continue to stay indefinitely if circumstances dictated.

The question of free will versus determinism is huge, of course. In the one reality, every pair of opposites is ultimately an illusion. We've already blurred the division between *good and evil* and life and death. Is free will going to turn out to be the same as determinism? A lot seems to ride on the answer.

FREE WILL =

Independence

Self-determination

Choice

Control over events

Future is open

DETERMINISM =

Dependence on an outside will
Self determined by fate
No control over events
Choices made for you
Future is closed

These phrases sketch in the common understanding of what's at stake. Everything in the free-will column sounds attractive. We all want to be independent; we want to make our own decisions; we want to wake up with hope that the future is open and full of endless possibilities. On the other hand, nothing seems attractive in the determination column. If your choices have been made for you, if your self is tied to a plan written before you were born, then the future cannot be open. Emotionally at least, the prospect of free will has already won the argument.

And at a certain level nobody has to delve any deeper. If you and I are marionettes operated by an invisible puppeteer—call him God, fate, or karma—then the strings he's pulling are also invisible. We have no proof that we aren't making free choices, except for the occasional spooky moments of the kind I began with, and mind-readers aren't going to change how we fundamentally behave.

There is a reason to delve deeper, however, and it centers on the word *Vasana*. In Sanskrit, a Vasana is an unconscious cause. It's the software of the psyche, the driving force that makes you do something when you think you're doing it spontaneously. As such, Vasana is very disturbing. Imagine a robot whose every action is driven by a software program inside. From the robot's point of view, it doesn't matter that the program exists—until something goes wrong. The illusion of not being a robot collapses if the software breaks down because then, if the robot wants to do something but can't, we know the reason why.

Vasana is determinism that feels like free will. I'm reminded of my friend Jean, whom I've known for almost twenty years. Jean considers himself very spiritual and went so far in the early nineties as to walk way from his job with a newspaper in Denver to live in an ashram in western Massachusetts. But he found the atmosphere choking. "They're all crypto Hindus," he complained. "They don't do anything but pray and chant and meditate." So Jean decided to move on with his life. He's fallen in love with a couple of women but has never married. He doesn't like the notion of settling down and tends to move to a new state every four years or so. (He once told me that he counted up and discovered that he's lived in forty different houses since he was born.)

One day Jean called me with a story. He was on a date with a woman who had taken a sudden interest in Sufism, and while they were driving home, she told Jean that according to her Sufi teacher, everyone has a prevailing characteristic.

"You mean the thing that is most prominent about them, like being extroverted or introverted?" he asked.

"No, not prominent," she said. "Your prevailing characteristic is hidden. You act on it without seeing that you're acting on it."

The minute he heard this, Jean became excited. "I looked out the car window, and it hit me," he said. "I sit on the fence. I am only comfortable if I can have both sides of a situation without committing to either." All at once a great many pieces fell into place. Jean could see why he went into an ashram but didn't feel like he was one of the group. He saw why he fell in love with women but always saw their faults. Much more came to light. Jean complains about his family yet never misses a Christmas with them. He considers himself an expert on every subject he's studied—there have been many—but he doesn't earn his living pursuing any of them. He is indeed an inveterate fence-sitter. And as his date suggested, Jean had no idea that his Vasana, for that's what we're talking about, made him enter into one situation after another without ever falling off the fence.

"Just think," he said with obvious surprise, "the thing that's the most me is the thing I never saw."

If unconscious tendencies kept working in the dark, they wouldn't be a problem. The genetic software in a penguin or wildebeest guides it to act without any knowledge that it is behaving much like every other penguin or wildebeest. But human beings, unique among all living creatures, want to break down Vasana. It's not good enough to be a pawn who thinks he's a king. We crave the assurance of absolute freedom and its result—a totally open future. Is this reasonable? Is it even possible?

In his classic text, the *Yoga Sutras,* the sage Patanjali informs us that there are three types of Vasana. The kind that drives pleasant behavior he calls white Vasana; the kind that drives unpleasant behavior he calls dark Vasana; the kind that mixes the two he calls mixed Vasana. I would say Jean had mixed Vasana—he liked fence-sitting but he missed the reward of lasting love for another person, a driving aspiration, or a shared vision that would bond him with a community. He displayed the positives and negatives of someone who must keep every option open. The goal of the spiritual aspirant is to wear down Vasana so that clarity can be achieved. In clarity you know that you are not a puppet—you have released yourself from the unconscious drives that once fooled you into thinking that you were acting spontaneously.

The secret here is that the state of release isn't free will. Free will is the opposite of determinism, and in the one reality, opposites must ultimately merge into one. In the case of life versus death, we saw that they merged because both are needed to renew the flow of experience. Free will and determinism don't merge like that. They merge only when a cosmic argument is settled once and for all. Here is the argument in its simplest form.

There are two claims to ultimate reality. One claim comes from the physical world, where events have definite causes and effects. The other claim comes from absolute Being, which has no cause. Only one claimant can be right because there's no such thing as two ultimate realities. So which is it?

If the physical world is the ultimate reality, then you have no choice but to play out the game of Vasana. Every tendency has a cause in a prior tendency, and as soon as you wear out one, you will be creating another to replace it. You can't be a finished product. There is always something waiting to be fixed, attended to, adjusted, polished, cleaned up, or ready to fall apart. (People who can't face this fact turn into perfectionists, constantly chasing the chimera of a flawless existence. Although they don't realize it, they are trying to defeat the law of Vasana, which dictates that no cause can disappear; it can only transform itself into a new cause.) The physical world is also called the domain of karma, which has its own cosmic side. *Karma,* as we know, means "action," and the question to ask of action is this: Did it have a beginning? Does it ever end? Every person who was ever born found himself thrown into a world of action that was already fully operational. There is no hint that a first action got things started, and no way to tell if a last action might bring everything to a halt. The universe is a given, and despite theories about the Big Bang, the possibility of other universes, or even infinite universes, means that the chain of first events could extend forever.

The ancient sages didn't bother with telescopes because they saw, in a flash of insight, that the mind is ruled by cause and effect and therefore it doesn't have the power to look beyond karma. The thought I have right now emerged from the thought I had a second ago. The thought I had a second ago emerged from a thought I had the second before that—and on and on. Big Bang or not, my mind is a prisoner of karma because thinking is all it can do.

There is one alternative, the sages argued. Your mind can be. This is how the second claimant got into court. The ultimate reality could be Being itself. Being doesn't act; therefore, it is never touched by karma. If Being is the ultimate reality, the game of Vasana is over. Instead of worrying about cause and effect, which is the origin of all tendencies, one can simply say *there is no cause and effect.*

I said that Vasana gave us a reason to delve deeper into free will. Now we can see why. The person who is content to remain a puppet is no different from the rebel who screams that he must remain free at all costs. Both are subject to karma; their opinions make no difference to the matter. But if you can identify with a state that has no Vasanas, free will and determinism merge; they become mere instructions in the manual of karmic software. In other words, both are tools to be used by Being rather than ends in themselves. Karma, it turns out, loses the argument about being the ultimate reality.

How can I say that the argument is settled? I could say it's settled by authority because the spiritual record holds countless sages and saints who testify that Being is the ultimate ground of existence. But since we aren't relying on authority here, the proof has to come from experience. I experience that I am alive, which seems to help the case for karma, since being alive consists of one action after another. But I cannot be alive if the whole universe isn't alive. This conclusion would seem absurd without building up to it. But we have come far enough to realize that the real absurdity is to be alive in a dead universe. No one before modern times felt that he or she was stranded on a speck of rock and water with nothing but a black void to look out at. I find that image, which underlies the superstition of science, horrifying and untrue. My body and the universe are composed of the same molecules, and no matter how hard I try, I can't manage to believe that a hydrogen atom is alive inside me but dead the instant it leaves my lungs.

My body and the universe come from the same source, obey the same rhythms, flash with the same storms of electromagnetic activity. My body can't afford to argue over who created the universe. Every cell would disappear the second it stopped creating itself. So it must be that the universe is living and breathing through me. I am an expression of everything in existence.

At any given moment, the bubbling subatomic activity that keeps the universe going is in flux; every particle winks in and out of existence thousands of times per second. In that interval, I also wink in and out, traveling from existence to annihilation and back again billions of times a day. The universe came up with this lightning-fast rhythm so that it could pause in between and decide what to create next. The same is true of me. Even though my mind works too slowly to see the difference, I'm not the same person after I return from my billion journeys into the void. Every single process in my cells has been rethought, reexamined, reorganized. Creation happens by infinitesimal degrees, and the overall result is eternal genesis.

In a living universe, we do not have to answer any questions about who the creator is. At various times, religions have named a single god, multiple gods and goddesses, an invisible life force, a cosmic mind, and in the current religion of physics, a blind game of chance. Choose any or all of these because what's far more crucial about genesis is you. Can you see yourself as the point around which everything is now revolving?

Look around and try to view your whole situation. From the viewpoint of a limited self, you cannot be the center of the cosmos. But that's because you are looking at karma. Your attention is going to bits and pieces of your situation—a current relationship, events at work, finances, perhaps tossing in a vague concern with some political crisis or the state of the stock market. No matter how many of these ingredients you try to comprehend, you aren't seeing your whole situation. From the perspective of wholeness, the universe is thinking *about you*. Its thoughts are invisible, but they eventually manifest as tendencies—the by now familiar Vasanas—and sometimes your attention feels the larger design at work because every life has inescapable turning points, opportunities, epiphanies, and breakthroughs.

To you, a thought is an image or idea floating through your mind. To the universe—and here we mean the universal intelligence that permeates the swarm of galaxies, black holes, and interstellar dust—a thought is a step in evolution. It's a creative act. To truly live at the center of the one reality, evolution must become of primary interest to you. The noncritical events in your life already run themselves. Think of your body, which operates with two separate types of nervous system. The involuntary nervous system is automatic—it regulates the everyday functions of the body without intervention from you. When someone goes into a coma, this nervous system continues more or less normally, keeping heartbeat, blood pressure, hormones, electrolytes, and a hundred other functions going in perfect coordination.

The other nervous system is called voluntary because it relates to will, or volition. The voluntary nervous system carries out desires. That is its only purpose, and without it, life would run exactly as it does for someone in a coma, without any motion forward, frozen in a waking death.

The universe reflects the same division. On one level, natural forces need no assistance from us to keep everything regulated so that life can be sustained. Ecology is self-balancing. Plants and animals exist in harmony without knowing that they do. One could imagine a world in which nothing expands beyond basic existence, where instead creatures are reduced to eating, breathing, and sleeping. Such a world doesn't exist, however. Even one-celled amoebas swim in a particular direction, hunt for food, move toward light, and seek temperatures they prefer. Desire is built into the scheme of life.

So it's not that incredible to look for the second half of the universe's nervous system, the half that revolves around desire. When your brain carries out a desire, the universe is carrying it out at the same time. There is no difference between "I want to have a child" and "The universe wants to have a child." The embryo that starts to grow in the womb relies on billions of years of intelligence, memory, creativity, and evolution. The individual seamlessly flows into the cosmos when we are talking about fetuses in the womb. Why should this merging stop there? The fact that you experience your desire as individual doesn't negate the universe from acting through you, just as the fact that you consider your children to be yours doesn't negate the fact that they are also the children of a vast gene pool. That gene pool has no other parent than the universe.

At this moment, you are seamlessly flowing with the cosmos. There is no difference between your breathing and the breathing of the rain forest, between your bloodstream and the world's rivers, between your bones and the chalk cliffs of Dover. Every shift in the ecosystem has affected you at the level of your genes. The universe remembers its evolution by leaving a record written in DNA. This means that your genes are the focal point for everything happening in the world. They are your line of communication with nature as a whole, not just with your mother and father.

Set aside what you have read about DNA as a string of sugars and amino acids strung in a double helix. That model tells us what DNA looks like, but it says almost nothing about what is actually going on in the dynamics of life, just as the wiring diagram of a television tells us nothing about what's playing on the screen. What's playing through your DNA at this moment is the evolution of the universe. The next desire you have will be recorded in memory, and either the universe will move forward or it won't. We tend to think of evolution as a straight-line march from primitive organisms to higher ones. A better image would be of a bubble expanding to take in more and more of life's potential.

- As you access *more intelligence,* you are evolving. On the other hand, if you constrict your mind to what you already know or can predict, your evolution will slow down.

- As you access *more creativity,* you are evolving. On the other hand, if you try to use old solutions to solve new problems, your evolution will slow down.

- As you access *more awareness,* you are evolving. On the other hand, if you continue to use a fraction of your consciousness, your evolution will slow down.

The universe has a stake in which choices you decide to make, for the overwhelming evidence is that it favors evolution over standing still. In Sanskrit, the evolutionary force is called *Dharma,* from a root word that means "to uphold." Without you, Dharma would be confined to three dimensions. Even though you spend almost no time thinking about your relationship to a zebra, a coconut tree, or blue-green algae, each is your intimate in the evolutionary scheme. Human beings extended the evolutionary scheme when life reached a certain limit in physicality—after all, in physical terms, the earth depends on blue-green algae and plankton more than on humans. The universe wanted to have a new perspective, and for this had to *create creators* like itself.

I once asked a physicist if everyone in his community accepted by now that reality was nonlocal. He conceded that they did. "Isn't nonlocality the same as omniscience?" I said. "There's no distance in time, no distance in space. Communication is instantaneous, and every particle is connected to every other."

"Could be," he said, not exactly agreeing but letting me go on.

"Then why did the universe bother to become local?" I said. "It already knew everything. It already includes everything, and at the deepest level it already encompasses all events that could possibly happen."

"I don't know," my physicist said. "Maybe the universe just wanted a vacation."

This isn't a bad answer. Through us the universe gets to play. Play at what? At giving someone else the controls to see what he or she comes up with. The one thing the universe can't experience is getting away from itself. So, in a sense, we are its vacation.

The problem with dilemmas like free will and determinism is that they don't leave enough playtime. This is a recreational universe. It provides us with food, air, water, and a great deal of scenery to explore. All of that comes from the automatic side of cosmic intelligence. It continues on its own, but the side that wants to play is plugged into evolution, and Dharma is its way of telling us how the game works. If you look carefully at the critical turning points in your life, you'll see how closely you were paying attention to the evolutionary game.

BEING IN THE DHARMA

- You were *ready to move forward.* The experience of your old reality was worn out and ready for change.
- You were *ready to pay attention.* When the opportunity arrived, you noticed it and took the necessary leap.
- The *environment supported you.* When you moved forward, events fell into place to ensure that you didn't backslide.
- You *felt more expanded and free* in your new place.
- You saw yourself as in some way *a new person.*

This set of circumstances, both inner and outer, is what Dharma provides. Which is to say that when you feel ready to move forward, reality shifts to show you how. And when you aren't ready to move forward? Then there is the backup system of Vasana, which moves you forward by repeating those tendencies that are embedded in you from the past. When you find yourself stuck and unable to make any progress at all, the following circumstances usually apply:

1. *You aren't ready to move.* The experience of an old reality still fascinates you. You keep enjoying your habitual way of life, or else, if there is more pain than enjoyment, you are addicted to the pain for some reason not yet revealed.

2. *You aren't paying attention.* Your mind is caught up in distractions. This is especially true if there is too much external stimulation. Unless you feel alert inside, you won't be able to pick up the hints and clues being sent from the one reality.

3. *The environment won't support you.* When you try moving forward, circumstances push you back. This kind of thwarting means that there is more to learn, or that the timing isn't yet right. It also can be true that at a deep level you don't see yourself moving forward; your conscious desire is in conflict with deeper doubt and uncertainty.

4. *You feel threatened* by the expansion you would have to make, preferring the safety of a limited self-image. Many people cling to a contracted state, believing that it protects them. In fact, the greatest protection you could ask for comes from evolution, which solves problems by expansion and forward movement. But you must own this knowledge completely; if any part of you

wants to hang back in a constricted state, that's usually enough to block the road ahead.

5. *You keep seeing yourself as the old person* who adapted to an old situation. This is often an unconscious choice. People identify with their past and try to use old perceptions to understand what is happening. Since perception is everything, seeing yourself as too weak, limited, undeserving, or lacking will block any step forward.

The full implication is that Dharma needs you to collaborate. The upholding force is as much in you as it is "out there" in the universe or the realm of the soul.

The single best way to align with the Dharma is to assume that it is listening. Give the universe room to respond to you. Start up a relationship with it as with another person. I have been a doting grandfather for two years now, and I'm astonished that my granddaughter Tara has no problem talking to trees, rocks, the ocean, or the sky. She takes for granted that there is subjectivity everywhere. "See those dragons?" she'll say, pointing to an empty space in the middle of the living room, naming a blue dragon here and a red one there. I ask Tara if she is afraid of the dragons, but she assures me that they've always been friendly.

Children inhabit imaginary worlds, not for the sake of pure fantasy but to test their creative instincts. Tara is a creator in training, and if deprived of her relationship to trees, rocks, and dragons, she would be cut off from a power that needs to grow. At her age Tara's life is all playtime, and in the role of grandfather I try to immerse her in as much love and pleasure as possible. Her Vasana is going to be white if I can help it. But I also know that the great challenge for her will be to go beyond every tendency, good or bad. She will have to remain alert to stay in the Dharma, and for those of us who grew up to find that life is a serious business with few time-outs for play, the Dharma awaits our return to sanity.

CHANGING YOUR REALITY TO ACCOMMODATE THE ELEVENTH SECRET

The eleventh secret is about escaping the bondage of cause and effect. The universe is alive, and imbued with subjectivity. Cause and effect are just the machinery it uses to carry out what it wants to do. And what it wants to do is to live and breathe through you. To find out the truth of this, you need to relate to the universe as if it were alive. Otherwise, how will you ever know that it is? Today, begin to adopt the following habits:

Talk to the universe.
Listen for its reply.
Be on intimate terms with Nature.
See the life in everything.
Carry yourself like a child of the universe.

The first step, talking to the universe, is the most important. It doesn't imply that you go around muttering to the stars or that you begin an imaginary cosmic conversation. The habit of looking at the world "out there" as disconnected from you is entrenched; we all share a cultural bias that reserves life only for plants and animals, and that places intelligence exclusively in the brain. You can begin to break down this belief by acknowledging any hint that the inner and outer worlds are connected. Both have the same source; both are organized by the same deep intelligence; both respond to each other.

When I say that you can talk to the universe, I mean you can connect to it. If you feel depressed by a gray and rainy day, for example, see the inner and outer grayness as the same phenomenon with objective and subjective sides. If you are driving home from work and your gaze is caught by a glowing sunset, consider that Nature wanted to catch your attention, not that you and the sunset are having just an accidental encounter. On some intimate level, your existence meshes with the universe, not by chance but by intention.

When you see the life that exists everywhere, acknowledge what you're seeing. At first, it may seem peculiar to do this, but you are a co-creator, and you have the right to appreciate the patterns of connection that you've made. Carrying yourself like a child of the universe isn't a game of cosmic pretend. At the level of the field, you exist everywhere in spacetime, a scientific fact that we are carrying a step further by saying that this moment in spacetime has a special purpose in your world. It is *your* world, and by responding to it that way, you will begin to notice that it responds back:

On some days everything goes right.
On some days everything goes wrong.
At certain moments you feel absorbed into the rhythm of Nature.
At some moments you feel as if you disappear into the sky or
the ocean.
Sometimes you know that you have always been here.

These are general examples, but you can be alert to moments that seem meant just for you. Why do certain moments feel uniquely magical? Only you will know, but you won't if you don't first begin to attune yourself to the feeling. The closest parallel I can draw to this kind of privileged relationship is that between lovers, in which ordinary moments are suffused with a presence or specialness that wouldn't be felt by an outsider. Something totally compelling draws your attention when you are in love; once experienced, it is not easily forgotten. You feel as if you are inside your beloved and your beloved is inside you. The merging of yourself with something vaster than yourself is a blending of two subjectivities. It's been called the relationship of "I and thou," or the sense of being as a wave on the infinite ocean of Being.

Don't let names and concepts distract you. There's no defined way for you to relate to the universe. Just relate in your own way. A little child like my granddaughter finds her way in talking to trees and invisible dragons. That's her privileged relationship. What is yours going to be? Shiver with anticipation and find out.

❀

THERE IS NO
TIME BUT NOW

THERE HAVE BEEN MOMENTS when my whole life made sense. I knew exactly who I was. The people in my life were all there for a reason. Clearly, and without a shred of doubt, I knew that the reason was love, so for that moment I could laugh at the preposterous notion that I had enemies or that I was a stranger in this world.

Perfection has a mysterious way of slipping in and out of time. Few people, I imagine, haven't felt the kind of moment I just described, but I've never met a single person who could hold on to it. But people desperately want to, and often this hunger motivates their spiritual life. In the Buddhist tradition, there are a wealth of exercises devoted to mindfulness, a state of awareness in which you can be conscious of perfect moments. Let's hope they all become perfect. But to be aware, you must first catch yourself being *unaware*, which is difficult; after all, being unaware can be defined as not knowing that you aren't aware.

I had a hard time with this slipperiness until someone told me, "It's like being happy. When you're happy, you're just happy. You don't have to think about it. But then a moment comes when you say out loud, 'I really feel happy right now,' and it starts to disappear. In fact, you can break the spell simply by thinking the words 'I'm happy right now' to yourself."

That one example explained to me what it means to be mindful: You catch the present moment without words or thought. Few things are easier to describe and harder to do. The crux of the matter is time. Time is as slippery as that blessed moment before you say "I'm happy right now." Was that moment really fleeting or is it eternal?

Most of us take for granted that time flies, meaning that it passes too quickly. But in the mindful state, time doesn't really pass at all. There is only a single instant of time that keeps renewing itself over and over with infinite variety. The secret about time, then, is that it exists only as we usually think of it. Past, present, and future are only mental boxes for things we want to keep close or far from us, and by saying that "time flies," we conspire to prevent reality from coming too close. Is time a myth we are using for our own convenience?

Books are written extolling the virtues of living in the present moment. There is good reason for this because the mind's burdens come from the past. By itself, memory is weightless, and time should be, too. What people call "the now" is actually the disappearance of time as a psychological obstacle. When the obstacle is removed, you are no longer burdened by the past or the future—you've found the mindful state (and happiness, too—the kind that needs neither words nor thoughts). What makes time a psychological burden is ourselves—we have convinced ourselves that experiences are built up over time.

I'm older than you, I know what I'm talking about.
I've been around the block a few times.
Listen to the voice of experience.
Pay attention to your elders.

These formulas make a virtue out of experience accumulated not with insight or alertness but simply by hanging around. Mostly they are futile expressions, however. We all know at some level that carrying around a heavy suitcase of time is what makes people gray.

To live in the present moment means dropping the suitcase, not carrying it with you. But how is this done? In the one reality, the only time on the clock is now. The trick to dropping the past is to find out how to live now as if it were forever. Photons move at Planck time, which matches the speed of light, while galaxies evolve over billions of years. So if time is a river, it must be a very deep one and broad enough to contain the least speck of time and the infinity of timelessness.

This implies that "now" is more complex than it looks. Are you in the now when you are most active and energized, or when you are most still? Take a look at a river. On the surface, the current is fast and restless. At the middle depths, the flow slows down, until one reaches the bottom, where the silt is only slightly stirred before you touch bedrock, where the motion of water no longer has any effect. The mind is capable of participating at every level of the river. You can run with the fastest current, which most people try to do in their everyday lives. Their version of now is whatever has to be done *right now.* For them, the present moment contains constant drama. Time equals action, just as it does on the surface of the river.

When they become exhausted from the race (or feel that they are losing it) people in a hurry may finally slow down, only to be surprised at how hard it actually is to go from running to walking. But if you decide, "Okay, I'll just keep going," life brings new problems, such as obsessions, circular thinking, and so-called racing depression. In a sense, these are all disorders of time.

Tagore has a wonderful phrase for this: "We're too poor to be late." In other words, we race through life as if we can't afford to throw away a single minute. In the same poem, Tagore gives a perfect description of what you find after all the rushing around gets where it wants to go:

> *And when the frantic race was over*
> *I could see the finish line*
> *Bursting with fear lest I be too late*
> *Only to find at the last minute*
> *That yet there is time.*

Tagore is reflecting on what it means to race through your life as if you haven't time to spare, only to find at the end that you always had eternity. But our minds have a hard enough time adjusting to a slower pace when they are so conditioned to misusing time. An obsessive-compulsive person, for example, is typically panicked by the clock. There is barely enough time to clean the house twice before company comes, barely enough time to line up forty pairs of shoes in the closet and still make dinner. Where did time go wrong?

Without being able to locate the source of obsession, psychologists have discovered that low self-esteem is accompanied by negative words like *lazy, dull, stupid, ugly, loser, worthless,* and *failure* that get repeated *several hundred times per hour.* This rapid-fire repetition is both a symptom of mental suffering and a futile attempt to find a cure. The same word keeps coming back over and over because the person desperately wants it to go away and yet has not discovered how to expunge it.

Circular thinking is related to obsession, but with more steps involved. Instead of chewing over a single notion like "the house isn't clean enough" or "I have to be perfect," the person is imprisoned in false logic. An example would be someone who feels unlovable. No matter how much people express love for them, the circular thinkers do not feel lovable because inside their minds they are saying, "I want to get love, and this person is saying he loves me, but I can't feel it, which must mean I am unlovable, and the only way I can fix that is to get love." Circular logic afflicts those who never become successful enough, never feel safe enough, never feel wanted enough. The initial premise that drives them to act ("I'm a failure," "I'm in danger," "I'm in need") doesn't change because every result from the outside, whether good or bad, reinforces the original idea. These examples bring us to the "paradox of now": The faster you run in place, the further you are from the present moment.

Racing depression gives us a very clear picture of the paradox because depressed people do feel inert, trapped in a frozen dead moment without any feeling except hopelessness. For them, time is standing still, and yet their minds race with shredded ideas and emotions. This flurry of mental activity doesn't seem like what should be going on in the head of someone who can't get out of bed in the morning. But in this case, the mental flurry is disconnected from action. A depressed person thinks of countless things but acts on none of them.

When these problems aren't present, the mind slows down by diving deeper. People who take time out for themselves are seeking the calm of solitude, where external demands are fewer. In its natural state, the mind stops reacting once external stimulation goes away. This is like escaping the waves in the river's shallows to find a depth where the current slows down. The present moment becomes a kind of lazy circular eddy. Your thoughts keep moving, but they aren't so insistent that they push you forward.

Finally, there are a few people who enjoy stillness more than activity, and they dive as deep as they can to find where the water stops running, a point so still and deep that one isn't touched by the surface waves at all. Having found this stable center, they experience themselves to the maximum and the outside world to the minimum.

One way or another, we've all experienced these different versions of the present moment, from an exhausting race to motionless calm. But what about the now that is right before you, *this* now? In the one reality, this now has no duration—relative terms like *fast* and *slow, past* and *future,* don't apply. The present moment includes faster than the fastest and slower than the slowest. Only when you include the whole river are you living in the one reality, and then you're living in a state of awareness that is ever fresh and changeless.

So how do you get there?

To answer that, we have to look into relationships. When you meet someone you know well—let's say your best friend—what happens? The two of you perhaps meet at a restaurant to catch up, and your talk is full of old, familiar things, which feels reassuring. But you also want to say something new, or the relationship would be static and boring. You know each other extremely well already, which is part of being best friends, yet at the same time you aren't totally predictable to one another—the future will unfold new events, some happy, some sad. Ten years from now one of you could be dead or divorced or turned into a stranger.

This intersection of the new and the old, the known and the unknown, is the essence of all relationships, including the ones you have with time, the universe, and yourself. Ultimately, you are having only a single relationship. As you evolve, so does the universe, and the intersection of the two of you is time. There is only one relationship because there is only one reality. It's been a while since I referred to the four paths of Yoga, but each one is actually a flavor of relationship:

- The path of knowledge (Gyana Yoga) has a flavor of mystery. You sense the inexplicability of life. You experience the wonder inside every experience.

- The path of devotion (Bhakti Yoga) has the flavor of love. You experience the sweetness inside every experience.

- The path of action (Karma Yoga) has the flavor of selflessness. You experience the connectedness of every experience.

- The path of meditation and inner silence (Raj Yoga) has the flavor of stillness. You experience the being inside every experience.

Time exists so that you can experience these flavors as deeply as possible. On the path of devotion, if you can experience even a glimmer of love, it's possible to experience a little more love. When you experience that little more, then the next degree of intensity is possible. Thus, love engenders love until you reach the point of saturation, when you totally merge into divine love. This is what the mystics mean when they say that they plunge into the ocean of love to drown themselves.

Time unfolds the degrees of experience until you reach the ocean. Pick any quality that holds charm for you, and if you follow it far enough, with commitment and passion, you will merge with the absolute. For at the end of the path, each quality disappears, swallowed up by Being. Time isn't an arrow or a clock or a river; it's actually a fluctuation in the flavors of Being. Theoretically, nature could have been organized without a progression from less to more. You could experience love or mystery or selflessness at random. However, reality wasn't set up that way, at least not as experienced through a human nervous system. We experience life as evolving. Relationships grow from the first hint of attraction to deep intimacy. (Love at first sight takes the same journey but in a matter of minutes instead of weeks and months.) Your relationship to the universe follows the same course—if you let it. Time is meant to be the vehicle for evolution, but if you misuse time, it becomes a source of fear and anxiety.

THE MISUSE OF TIME

Being anxious about the future
Reliving the past
Regretting old mistakes
Reliving yesterday
Anticipating tomorrow
Racing against the clock
Brooding over impermanence
Resisting change

When you misuse time, the problem isn't at the level of time itself. Nothing has gone wrong with the clocks in the house of someone who loses five hours' sleep worrying about the possibility of dying from cancer. The misuse of time is only a symptom for misplaced attention. You can't have a relationship with someone you don't pay attention to, and in your relationship to the universe, attention is paid here and now, or not at all. In fact, there is no universe except the one you perceive right now. So to relate to the universe, you must focus on what lies in front of you. As one spiritual teacher said, "The wholeness of creation is needed to bring about the present moment."

If you take this to heart, your attention will shift. Right now, every situation you are in is a mixture of past, present, and future. Imagine yourself applying for a job. As you offer yourself to the scrutiny of a stranger, trying to handle the stress and make a good impression, you aren't actually in the now. "Will I get this job?" "How do I look?" "Were my recommendations good enough?" "What's this guy thinking, anyway?" It seems as if you can't help tumbling in the mix of past, present, and future. But the now can't be a mixture of old and new. It must be clear and open; otherwise, there is no unfolding of yourself, which is the reason time exists.

The present moment is really an opening, so it has no duration—you are in the now when time ceases to exist. Perhaps the best way to gain such an experience is to realize that the word *present* is linked to the word *presence.* When the present moment becomes filled with a presence that is all-absorbing, completely at peace, and totally satisfying, you are in the now.

Presence isn't an experience. Presence is felt whenever awareness is open enough. The situation at hand doesn't have to bear any responsibility. Paradoxically, someone can be in intense pain, only to find that in the middle of his suffering, the mind—unable to tolerate the body's torment—suddenly decides to abandon it. This is particularly true of psychological pain—soldiers caught in the terror of battle report a moment of liberation when intense stress is replaced by a rush of ecstatic release.

Ecstasy changes everything. The body is no longer heavy and slow; the mind stops experiencing its background music of sadness and fear. There is a dropping away of personality, replaced by the sweetness of nectar. This sweetness can linger a long time in the heart—some people say it can be tasted like honey in the mouth—but when it leaves, you know beyond doubt that you have lost the now. In the mind's scrapbook, you can insert a picture of perfect bliss, and that becomes like the first taste of ice cream, an unattainable goal you keep running after, only to find that ecstasy remains out of reach.

The secret of ecstasy is that you have to throw it away once you've found it. Only by walking away can you experience the present moment again, the place where presence lives. Awareness is in the now when it knows itself. If we take away the vocabulary of sweetness and bliss and nectar, the quality that is missing in most people's lives, the biggest thing that keeps them from being present, is sobriety. You have to be sober before you can be ecstatic. This isn't a paradox. What you're hunting for—call it presence, the now, or

206 @ Deepak Chopra

ecstasy—is totally out of reach. You cannot hunt it down, chase after it, command it, or persuade it to come to you. Your personal charms are useless here, and so are your thoughts and insights.

Sobriety begins by realizing, in all seriousness, that you have to throw away almost every strategy that you've been using to get what you want. If that's at all intriguing, then carry out your sober intent to release those futile strategies as follows:

SPIRITUAL SOBRIETY

Getting Serious About Being in the Present

Catch yourself not paying attention.
Listen to what you're actually saying.
Watch how you react.
Remove yourself from the details.
Follow the rise and fall of energy.
Question your ego.
Immerse yourself in a spiritual milieu.

These instructions could come directly from a ghost hunter's handbook, or the hunter of unicorns. The present moment is more elusive than either, but if you want to get there passionately enough, sobriety is the program you need to set up.

Not paying attention: The first step is neither mystical nor extraordinary. When you observe that you're not paying attention, don't indulge your wandering. Come back to where you are. Almost instantly you'll discover why you wandered away. You were either bored, anxious, insecure, worrying about something else, or anticipating a future event. Don't evade any of those feelings. They are ingrained habits of awareness, habits you have trained yourself to follow automatically. When you catch yourself drifting away from what's right in front of you, you begin to take back the now.

Listening to what you're saying: Having returned from your distraction, listen to the words you're saying, or the ones in your head. Relationships are driven forward with words. If you listen to yourself, you will know how you are relating to the universe right now. Don't be thrown off by the fact that there is another person in front of you. Whoever you are talking to, including yourself, stands in for reality itself. If you are complaining about a lazy waiter, you are complaining about the universe. If you are showing off to someone you want to impress, you are trying to impress the universe. There is only one relationship. Listen to how it's going at this moment.

Watch your reaction: Every relationship is two-way, so whatever you are saying, the universe is responding. Watch your reaction. Are you defensive? Are you accepting and moving forward? Do you feel safe or unsafe? Again, don't be distracted by the person you are relating to. You are tuning in to the universe's response, closing the circle that embraces observer and observed.

Remove yourself from the details: Before sobriety, you had to find a way to adapt to the loneliness that comes from the absence of reality. Reality is wholeness. It is all-embracing. You dive in and there is nothing else. In the absence of wholeness you still crave a similar embrace, so you try to find it in fragments, bits and pieces. In other words, you tried to lose yourself in the details, as if sheer chaos and raucousness could saturate you to the point of fulfillment. Now you know that this strategy didn't work, so back out of it. Remove yourself from the details. Forget the messiness. Take care of it as efficiently as possible, but don't take it seriously; don't make it important to who you are.

Follow the rise and fall of energy: Once the details are out of the way, you still need something to follow. Your attention wants to go somewhere, so take it to the heart of experience. The heart of experience is the universe's breathing rhythm as it pours forth new situations, a rise and fall of energy. Notice how tension leads to release, excitement to fatigue, exhilaration to peace. Just as there is an ebb and flow in every marriage, your relationship to the universe rises and falls. You may experience these swings emotionally at first, but try not to. This is a much more profound rhythm. It begins in silence as a new experience is conceived; it moves through a period of gestation as the experience takes shape in silence; it begins to move toward birth by hinting at how things are going to change; finally there is the arrival of something new. This "something" can be a person in your life, an event, a thought, an insight—anything, really. Common to all is the rise and fall of energy. You need to connect with every stage because in the present moment one of them is right in front of you.

Question your ego: All this watching and noticing and catching yourself isn't going unnoticed. Your ego has its own "right" way of doing things, and when you break that pattern, it will let you know of its displeasure. Change is frightening, but more than that, it is threatening to the ego. This fright is just a tactic to pull you back into line. You can't fight your ego's reactions because that will only deepen your involvement with it. But you can question it, which means questioning yourself from a calm distance. "Why am I doing this?" "Isn't this a knee-jerk reflex?" "How far have I gotten in the past acting like this?" "Haven't I proved to myself that this doesn't work?" You must keep asking these stubborn questions over and over, with the intent not of breaking down your ego but of loosening its reflexive hold over your behavior.

Immerse yourself in a spiritual milieu: When you seriously face your behavior, you'll realize that the ego has been isolating you all along. It wants you to think that life is lived in separation because, with that belief, it can rationalize grabbing as much for I, me, and mine as it can. In much the same way, the ego tries to grab spirituality as if it were a prized new possession. To counter that tendency, which will lead only to more isolation, immerse yourself in another world. I'm referring to the world where people consciously pursue experiences of presence, where there's a common vision of transforming duality into unity. You can find such an environment in the great spiritual texts.

As someone who found untold hope and consolation in such writings, I can't urge you more strongly to turn to them. But there is a living world to meet as well. Immerse yourself in a spiritual context, according to how you define *spirit*. Expect to be disappointed when you get there, too, because it's inevitable that you will meet the most frustration among people struggling with their imperfections. The ferment you meet is your own.

Once you commit yourself to being sober, there is nothing more to do. Presence will appear on its own, and when it does, your awareness cannot help but be in the now. A moment in the now causes an internal change felt in every cell. Your nervous system is being taught a way of processing reality that isn't old or new, known or unknown. You rise to a new level of being in which presence matters for itself alone, and it matters absolutely. Every other experience is relative and therefore can be rejected, forgotten, discounted, put out of mind. Presence is the touch of reality itself, which cannot be rejected or lost. Each encounter makes you a little more real.

Evidence of this comes in many ways, the most immediate of which has to do with time itself. When the only time on the clock is now, the following becomes your actual experience:

1. The past and the future exist only in imagination. Everything you did before has no reality. Everything you will do afterward has no reality. Only the thing you are doing now is real.

2. The body you once called yourself is not who you are anymore. The mind you once called yourself is not who you are anymore.

You step out of them easily, without effort. Both are temporary patterns that the universe took for an instant before moving on.

3. Your actual self manifests at this moment as thoughts, emotions, and sensations passing across the screen of awareness. You recognize them as the meeting point between change and timelessness. You see yourself as exactly that also.

When you find yourself in the present moment, there is nothing to do. The river of time is allowed to flow. You experience the eddies and currents, shallows and depths, in a new context: innocence. The present moment is naturally innocent. The now turns out to be the only experience that doesn't go anywhere. How can this be true when I've said that the whole purpose of time is to unfold the steps of evolution? That's the mystery of mysteries. We grow and yet life remains eternal at the core. Imagine a universe expanding through infinite dimensions at infinite speed, completely free to create everywhere at once. To go along for the ride we need do nothing but remain absolutely still.

CHANGING YOUR REALITY TO ACCOMMODATE THE TWELFTH SECRET

The twelfth secret is about how to use time. The best use of time is to reconnect to your being. The misuse of time comes down to the opposite: moving away from your being. There is always enough time to evolve because you and the universe are unfolding together. How can you prove that to yourself? One way is through a Sanskrit practice called *Sankalpa.* Any intention or thought that you put your will behind is a Sankalpa. Included in the term is the whole idea of means: Having made a wish or had a thought you want to come true, how do you actually get results? The answer depends a great deal on your relationship to time (the root word *kalpa* means "time").

- If timelessness is part of your being, the wish will come true spontaneously without delay. You have the power to play with time as you would any other part of your world.

- If timelessness has a tentative relationship to your being, some wishes will come true spontaneously, others won't. There will be delays and an uneasy sense that you might not get what you want. Your ability to play with time is shaky but developing.

- If timelessness has no relationship to your being, it will take work and determination to get what you want. You have no power over time. Instead of playing with it, you are subject to its inexorable march.

From these three broad categories one can project three different belief systems. Consider which one best applies to you.

1. *I am pressed for time.* There aren't enough hours in the day to accomplish everything I want. Other people make a lot of demands on my time, and it's all I can do to keep everything in balance. What I've gotten in life I've earned through hard work and determination. As far as I know, this is the road to success.

2. *I consider myself pretty lucky.* I've gotten to do a lot of the things I've always wanted to do. Although my life is busy, I find a way to make enough time for myself. Every once in a while things just fall into place on their own. Deep down, I expect my wishes to come true, but I am okay if they don't.

3. *I believe that the universe brings you whatever you need.* Certainly that's true in my life. I'm amazed to find that my every thought brings some response. If I don't get what I want, I realize that something inside me is blocking it. I spend time working on my inner awareness far more than struggling with outside forces.

212 @ Deepak Chopra

These are just snapshots of Sankalpa, but most people fall into one of these categories. They represent, again in a very general way, three stages of personal evolution. It's useful to know that they exist, for many people would find it hard to believe that there is any reality other than the first one, in which hard work and determination are the only keys to getting what you want.

Once you gain even a hint that wishes can come true without so much struggle, you can resolve to move to a new stage of growth. Growth is accomplished by awareness, yet you can resolve today to change your relationship to time:

I will let time unfold for me.
I will keep in mind that there's always enough time.
I will follow my own rhythm.
I will not misuse time by procrastination and delay.
I will not fear what time brings in the future.
I will not regret what time brought in the past.
I will stop racing against the clock.

Try to adopt just one of these resolves today and see how it changes your reality. Time isn't demanding, although we all act as if the clock rules our existence (or if it doesn't, we still keep a close watch on it). Time is meant to unfold according to your needs and wants. It will start to do that only if you give up the opposite belief—that time is in charge.

❀

YOU ARE TRULY FREE WHEN
YOU ARE NOT A PERSON

SEVERAL YEARS AGO IN A SMALL VILLAGE outside New
Delhi, I was sitting in a small, stuffy room with a very old man and
a young priest. The priest sat on the floor swaying back and forth as
he recited words inked on bark sheets that looked ancient. I listened,
having no idea what the priest was intoning. He was from the far
south and his language, Tamil, was foreign to me. But I knew he was
telling me the story of my life, past and future. I wondered how I got
roped into this and began to squirm.

It had taken strong persuasion from an old friend to get me to
the small room. "It's not just Jyotish, it's much more amazing," he
coaxed. Indian astrology is called *Jyotish,* and it goes back thousands
of years. Visiting your family astrologer is common practice everywhere in India, where people plan weddings, births, and even routine
business transactions around their astrological charts (Indira Gandhi
was a famous example of someone who followed Jyotish), but modern times have led to a fading away of tradition. I had chronically
avoided any brushes with Jyotish, being a child of modern India and
later a working doctor in the West.

But my friend prevailed, and I had to admit that I was curious about what was going to happen. The young priest, dressed in a wrapped skirt with bare chest and hair shiny with coconut oil—both marks of a southerner—didn't draw up my birth chart. Every chart he needed had already been drawn up hundreds of years ago. In other words, someone sitting under a palm tree many generations ago had taken a strip of bark, known as a *Nadi,* and inscribed my life on it.

These Nadis are scattered all over India, and it's pure chance to run across one that applies to you. My friend had spent several years tracking down just one for himself; the priest produced a whole sheaf for me, much to my friend's amazed delight. You have to come for the reading, he insisted.

Now the old man sitting across the table was interpreting in Hindi what the priest was chanting. Because of overlapping birth times and the vagaries of the calendar when we are speaking of centuries, Nadis can overlap, and the first few sheets didn't apply to me. But by the third sheet or so, the young priest with the sing-song voice was reading facts that were startlingly precise: my birth date, my parents' names, my own name and my wife's, the number of children we have and where they live now, the day and hour of my father's recent death, his exact name, and my mother's.

At first there seemed to be a glitch: The Nadi gave the wrong first name for my mother, calling her Suchinta, when in fact her name is Pushpa. This mistake bothered me, so I took a break and went to a phone to ask her about it. My mother told me, with great surprise, that in fact her birth name was Suchinta, but since it rhymed with the word for "sad" in Hindi, an uncle suggested that it be changed when she was three years old. I hung up the phone, wondering what this whole experience meant, for the young priest had also read out that a relative would intervene to change my mother's name. No one in our family had ever mentioned this incident, so the young priest wasn't indulging in some kind of mind-reading.

For the benefit of skeptics, the young priest had passed nearly his whole life in a temple in South India and did not speak English or Hindi. Neither he nor the old man knew who I was. Anyway, in this school of Jyotish, the astrologer doesn't take down your birth time and cast a personal chart which he then interprets. Instead, a person walks into a Nadi reader's house, the reader takes a thumb-print, and based on that, the matching charts are located (always keeping in mind that the Nadis may be lost or scattered to the winds). The astrologer reads out only what someone else has written down perhaps a thousand years ago. Here's another twist to the mystery: Nadis don't have to cover everyone who will ever live, only those individuals who will one day show up at an astrologer's door to ask for a reading!

In rapt fascination I sat through an hour of more arcane information about a past life I had spent in a South Indian temple, and how my transgressions in that lifetime led to painful problems in this one, and (after a moment's hesitation while the reader asked if I really wanted to know) the day of my own death. The date falls reassuringly far in the future, although even more reassuring was the Nadi's promise that my wife and children would lead long lives full of love and accomplishment.

I walked away from the old man and the young priest into the blinding hot Delhi sunshine, almost dizzy from wondering how my life would change with this new knowledge. It wasn't the details of the reading that mattered. I have forgotten nearly all of them, and I rarely think of the incident except when my eye falls on one of the polished bark sheets, now framed and kept in a place of honor in our home. The young priest handed it to me with a shy smile before we parted. The one fact that turned out to have a deep impact was the day of my death. As soon as I heard it, I felt both a profound sense of peace and a new sobriety that has been subtly changing my priorities ever since.

Reflecting on everything now, I wish there was another name for astrology, like "nonlocal cognition." Someone who lived centuries ago knew me better than I know myself. He saw me as a pattern in the universe playing itself out, linked to earlier patterns layer upon layer. I felt that with that piece of bark I received firsthand proof that I am not restricted to the body, mind, or experiences I call "me."

If you live at the center of one reality, you begin to witness patterns coming and going. At first, these patterns continue to feel personal. You create the patterns, and that brings a sense of attachment. But artists are famous for not collecting their own works; it is the act of creation itself that brings satisfaction. Once completed, the painting holds no more life; the juice has been squeezed out of it. The same holds true for the patterns we create. Experience loses its juice when you know that you created it.

The notion of detachment, which crops up in every Eastern spiritual tradition, troubles many people, who equate it with being passive and disinterested. But what's really implied is the same detachment any creator has once the work is done. Having created an experience and then lived it out, one finds that detachment comes naturally. It doesn't happen all at once, however. For a long time we remain fascinated by the play of duality with its constantly warring opposites.

Yet eventually one is ready to undergo the experience called *metanoia*—Greek for having a change of heart. Because the word cropped up so many times in the New Testament, it took on a more spiritual meaning. It signified changing your mind about leading a sinful life, then it gained the connotation of repentance, and finally it expanded to mean eternal salvation. Yet if you step outside the walls of theology, metanoia is very close to what we've been calling transformation. You shift your sense of self from local to nonlocal. Instead of calling any experience "mine," you see that every pattern in the universe is temporary. The universe keeps shuffling its basic

THE BOOK OF SECRETS ⊛ 217

material into new shapes, and for a time you have called one of those shapes "me."

Metanoia is the secret behind Nadi reading, I think. A long-ago seer looked inside himself and picked a ripple of consciousness that had the name Deepak attached to it. He wrote the name down along with other details that rippled out into spacetime. This implies a level of awareness that I should be able to reach inside myself. If I could see myself as a ripple in the field of light (*Jyotish* is Sanskrit for "light"), I would find the freedom that cannot be attained by remaining who I am inside my accepted boundaries. If my parents' names were known before my birth, and if my father's time of death could be reckoned generations before he was born, these preconditions are closed off to change.

True freedom occurs only in nonlocal awareness.

The ability to shift from local to nonlocal awareness is for me the meaning of redemption or salvation. You go to that place where the soul lives without having to die first. Rather than argue the metaphysics of this again, let me reduce the issue of nonlocality to something everyone is pursuing: happiness. To try to be happy is intensely personal, and therefore it's something we give over to the ego, whose sole goal is to make "me" happy. If it turns out that happiness lies outside "me," in the domain of nonlocal awareness, that would be a convincing argument for metanoia.

Happiness is a complex thing for human beings. We find it hard to experience happiness without being reminded of the things that could shatter it. Some of these things stick to us from our past as traumatic wounds; others are projections into the future as worries and anticipations of disaster.

It's no one's fault that happiness is elusive. The play of opposites is a cosmic drama, and our minds have been conditioned to fit into it. Happiness, as everyone knows, is too good to last. And this is true, as long as you define it as "my" happiness; by doing so you have already tied yourself to a wheel that must spin to the other side. Metanoia, or nonlocal awareness, solves this problem by transcending it because there is no other way. The elements making up your life are conflicting. Even if you could manipulate every element so that it consistently led to happiness, there is the subtle problem of imagined suffering.

Therapists spend years detaching people from all the things they imagine might go wrong with their lives, things that have nothing to do with actual circumstances.

This reminds me of an experience that occurred to a medical colleague when I was in training years ago. He had an anxious patient who came in every few months for a complete physical, terrified by the prospect of contracting cancer. The X-rays were always negative, but she continued to come back, each time as worried as before. Finally after many years, her X-ray did indeed confirm that she had a malignancy. With a triumphant look she cried, "See, I told you so!" Imagined suffering is as real as any other kind, and sometimes they merge.

The fact that anyone would cling to unhappiness as fiercely as others cling to happiness is baffling until you look more closely at local awareness. Local awareness is caught on the border between the ego and the universe. This is an anxious place. On the one hand, the ego operates as if it were in control. You navigate through the world on the unspoken assumption that you are important and that getting what you want matters. But the universe is vast and the forces of nature impersonal. The ego's sense of control and self-importance seem like a total illusion when you consider that human beings are barely a speck on the cosmic canvas. There is no security for the individual who senses deep down that he or she is pretending to be at the center of creation—the physical evidence of your unimportance is too overwhelming.

But is escape really possible? In its own domain, the ego says no. Your personality is a karmic pattern fiercely holding on to itself.

However, when you detach yourself from local awareness, you stop playing the ego's game—meaning that you step outside the whole problem of making "me" happy. The individual can't be crushed by the universe if there is no individual. As long as you attach your identity to even one small part of your ego-personality, everything else comes along. It's like walking into a theater and hearing an actor say the words "To be or not to be." Instantly you know the character, his history, and his tragic fate.

Actors can throw off one role and put on another without having to do more than make a quick mental adjustment. Remembering to be Hamlet instead of Macbeth isn't done one word at a time. You simply call the right character up. Moreover, when you change one character for another, you find yourself in a new place—Scotland instead of Denmark, a witch's camp beside the road instead of a castle by the North Sea.

One way to give up local awareness is to realize that you already have. When you go home for Thanksgiving, you probably find yourself falling automatically into the role of the child you once were. At work, you play a different role than when you go on vacation. Our minds are so good at storing totally conflicting roles that even small children know how to switch smoothly from one to the other. When candid cameras are set up to catch three-year-olds at play without adults around, parents are often shocked by the transformations they see before their eyes: The sweet, obedient, conciliatory child they knew at home can turn into a raging bully. Some child psychologists go so far as to claim that upbringing plays only a minor part in who we grow up to be. Two children raised under the same roof with the same parental attention can be so different outside the home as to be unrecognizable as siblings. But it would be more correct to say that growing children learn many roles simultaneously, and the role learned at home is only one of many—nor should we expect it to be otherwise.

If you can see this in yourself, then nonlocal awareness is only a step away. All you need to realize is that all your roles exist simultaneously. Just like an actor, you keep your personas in a place beyond space and time. Macbeth and Hamlet are simultaneously found inside an actor's memory. It takes hours to play them out on the stage, but their real home isn't a place where hours pass. In awareness, the whole role exists silently but is complete in every detail.

Likewise, you store your overlapping roles in a place that is more home to you than the stage where you play out the dramas. If you try to sort out these overlapping roles, you'll find none of them is you. You are the one who pushes the mental button to enable the role to spring to life. From your vast repertoire, you select situations that play out personal karma, each ingredient seamlessly fitting into place to provide the illusion of being an individual ego.

The real you is detached from any role, any scenery, any drama. In spiritual terms, detachment isn't an end unto itself—it develops into a kind of mastery. When you have this mastery, you can shift into nonlocal awareness anytime you want. This is what the *Shiva Sutras* mean by using memory without allowing memory to use you. You exercise detachment by stepping outside your memorized persona, and then the karma attached to any role no longer sticks. If you try to change your karma one piece at a time, you may achieve limited results, but the improved model of yourself will not be any more free than the unimproved one.

If there is really a secret to happiness, it can be found only at the source of happiness, which has the following characteristics:

THE SOURCE OF HAPPINESS IS . . .

Nonlocal
Detached

Impersonal
Universal
Beyond change
Made of essence

This list breaks down metanoia into its component parts. Metanoia originally meant a change of heart, and I think the same elements apply:

Nonlocal: Before you can have a change of heart, you must step outside yourself to get a larger perspective. The ego tries to narrow every issue down to "What will I get out of this?" When you reframe the question as "What will *we* get out of this?" or "What will everyone get out of this?" your heart will immediately feel less confined and constricted.

Detached: If you have a stake in a particular outcome, you can't afford a change of heart. The boundaries are drawn; everyone has chosen a side to be on. The ego insists that keeping your eye on the prize—meaning the result it wants—is all-important. But in detachment, you realize that many outcomes could be beneficial to you. You work toward the outcome you believe is right, yet you remain detached enough to shift when your heart tells you that you should.

Impersonal: Situations seem to happen to people, but in reality they unfold from deeper karmic causes. The universe unfolds to itself, bringing to bear every cause that needs to be included. Don't take this process personally. The working out of cause and effect is eternal. You are part of this rising and falling that never ends, and only by riding the wave can you ensure that the waves don't drown you. The ego takes everything personally, leaving no room for higher guidance or purpose. If you can, realize that a cosmic plan is unfolding and appreciate the incredibly woven tapestry for what it is, a design of unparalleled marvel.

Universal: One time, when I was trying hard to understand the Buddhist concept of ego death (a concept that seemed at the time very cold and heartless), someone eased my mind by saying, "It's not that you destroy who you are. You just expand the sense of 'I' from your little ego to the cosmic ego." That's a big proposition, but what I liked about this version is that nothing gets excluded. You start seeing every situation as belonging in our world, and even though that sense of inclusion may start out small—my family, my house, my neighborhood—it can grow naturally. The very fact that the ego finds it absurd to say my world, my galaxy, my universe implies that there is a shift at hand that it can't make on its own. The key idea is to keep in mind that awareness is universal, however confined your ego makes you feel at any given moment.

Beyond change: The happiness you are used to comes and goes. Instead of thinking of this as a well that runs dry, imagine the atmosphere. There's always humidity in the atmosphere, and sometimes it releases itself as rain. The days when it doesn't rain haven't made the humidity go away; it's always present in the air, waiting to precipitate as conditions change. You can take the same attitude toward happiness, which is always present in awareness without having to precipitate every moment—it shows itself as conditions change. People are different in their baseline of emotion, and some experience more cheerfulness, optimism, and contentment than others.

This variety expresses the diversity of creation. You can't expect the desert and the rain forest to behave the same. Yet these alterations in personal makeup are superficial. The same unchanging happiness can be accessed in everyone's awareness. Know that this is true, and don't use the ups and downs of your personal happiness as a reason for not journeying to the source.

Essence: Happiness is not a unique thing. It is one flavor of essence among many. One time, a disciple complained to his teacher that all the time spent on spiritual work hadn't made him happy.

"Your job right now isn't to be happy," the teacher swiftly replied. "Your job is to become real." Essence is real, and when you capture it, happiness follows because all the qualities of essence follow. Trying to be happy as an end in itself is limited; you will be fortunate just to meet your ego's requirements for a happy life. If instead you devote yourself to a total shift in awareness, happiness arrives as a gift freely bestowed by consciousness.

CHANGING YOUR REALITY TO ACCOMMODATE THE THIRTEENTH SECRET

The thirteenth secret is about personal freedom. You cannot be truly free if your interactions with the universe are personal because a person is a limited package. If you remain inside the package, so will your awareness. Today, start to act as if your influence extends everywhere. One of the most common sights in India, or anywhere else in the East, used to be saffron-robed monks in meditation before dawn. Many other people (my grandmother and mother among them) rise at the same early hour and go to the temple to pray. The point of this practice is that they are meeting the day before it begins.

To meet the day before it begins means that you are present when it is born. You open yourself to a possibility. Because there are not yet any events, the infant day is open, fresh, and new. It could turn into anything. The meditating monks and the people at prayer want to add their influence of consciousness at that critical moment, like being present for the beginning of a baby's life.

Today you can do the same thing. Wake up as early as you usually do—ideally you would perform this exercise at first light in a seated position, but you can do it lying in bed before you get up—and let your mind look forward to the day ahead. At first you will probably notice the residue of habit. You will see yourself going through your usual routine at work, the everyday duties surrounding your family and other obligations. Then you are likely to experience residues from yesterday: the project you haven't finished, the deadline coming up, an unresolved disagreement. Next you will likely experience the return of worries, whatever is hanging over your head at the moment.

Let all this move in and out of awareness as it wants to. Have the intention that you want this tangle of images and words to clear. Your ego is going to take care of all these habitual issues anyway. Keep looking at the day ahead, which is not a thing of images or thoughts since it is just being born. Get a feeling for it; try to meet it with your being.

After a few moments you'll notice that your mind is less inclined to jump out of bed. You will drift in and out of a fuzzy awareness—this means you have dived a bit deeper than the surface layer of mental restlessness. (Don't let yourself fall asleep again, however. When drowsiness arises, return to your intention of meeting the day.)

At this point you'll find that, instead of images, your mind settles into a rhythm of feelings. This state is more difficult to describe than images or voices. It's like a sense of how things are going to be, or a sensation of being ready for whatever will come. Don't look for anything dramatic. I'm not talking about premonitions and portents. You are having a simple experience: Your being is meeting the day at the level of incubation, where events are seeds getting ready to sprout. Your only purpose is to be there. You don't need to change anything; you don't have to attach yourself to judgments or opinions about what you think should unfold today. When you meet the day, you add the influence of your awareness in silence.

And what good is that? The effect occurs on a subtle level. It's like sitting next to a child's bed just as she falls asleep. Your presence is enough, without words or actions, to settle the child. A day needs to begin in a settled state, free of the residues and eddies of yesterday's activity. But you are also adding a subtle level of intention by meeting the day. You are intending to let life unfold as it will. You've showed up with open mind and open heart.

I've described this exercise in detail as a way of opening the path your mind may take. You won't find yourself exactly duplicating the stages being outlined, but the exercise has been successful if you touch, however briefly, on any of the following states of awareness:

- You feel new. This day is going to be unique.
- You feel at peace. This day is going to settle some stressful issue.
- You feel in harmony. This day is going to be free of conflict.
- You feel creative. This day is going to show you something never seen before.
- You feel loving. This day is going to soothe differences and include those who feel left out.
- You feel whole. This day is going to flow seamlessly.

Now you've been introduced to the predawn world where saints and sages have functioned for thousands of years. What they have been doing, and what you are now beginning to do, is to precipitate reality onto the earth. You are opening a channel in your own awareness through which renewal, peace, harmony, creativity, love, and wholeness get a chance to be here. Without someone to meet the day, these qualities exist only inside individuals—or sometimes not at all. Like rain falling out of a clear sky, your influence causes a possibility to become manifest.

THE MEANING OF LIFE
IS EVERYTHING

HAVE WE COME CLOSER to answering the ultimate question, "What is the meaning of life?" Imagine for a moment that someone came up with an answer. Directly or indirectly, most of the traditional answers have crossed everyone's path; the meaning of life usually comes down to a higher purpose, such as:

To glorify God
To glorify God's creation
To love and be loved
To be true to oneself

As with many other spiritual questions, I find it difficult to imagine how these answers could be tested. If someone holds down a good job, supports his or her family, pays taxes, and obeys the law, is that an example of glorifying God or of being true to oneself? In times of great crisis, such as war, does the meaning of life change? Perhaps it is all one can do to stay alive and be reasonably happy in a crisis.

One way to test the answer to the question "What is the meaning of life?" would be to write it down, seal it in an envelope, and mail it to a thousand people picked at random. If the answer is right, anyone who opens the envelope would read what is written and say, "Yes, you're right. That's the meaning of life." A breathless young bride would agree on her wedding day. A paralyzed old man would agree on his deathbed. People who war bitterly over differences in politics and religion would agree, and so would those who enjoy a marriage of the mind.

This might seem like an impossible test, however, since there might be absolutely no answer that would satisfy everyone. But what if the piece of paper is blank, or if it said, "The meaning of life is everything"? In the one reality, these aren't trick answers but very close to each other in reading the truth. The blank piece of paper indicates that life is pure potential until someone shapes it into something. The meaning of pure potential is that life is infinitely open. Similarly, to say that the meaning of life is everything indicates that life leaves nothing and no one out. "Everything" is just another way to embrace the infinite range of possibilities.

Life refuses to be pinned down. Whatever meaning you want the universe to reflect, it provides. In medieval Europe, people wanted the universe to reflect their intense belief in the Holy Trinity; at that same period in history, people in India wanted the universe to reflect the cosmic dance of Shiva and his consort Shakti. Wherever Islam held sway, the universe was expected to reflect the will of Allah. Right now, agnostics expect the universe to reflect their own spiritual confusion and doubt; therefore, the cosmos seems to be a random explosion that began with the Big Bang. Many religious people accept this reality, except on Sunday, when the universe feebly reflects the possibility of a divine maker.

If you try to pin the universe down to one reflection, you pin your own life down at the same time. Reality is like a two-way mirror that shows you yourself as well as what lies on the other side. This mutual effect is mandated because the universe doesn't possess one set of facts. You the observer bring your version of reality into being. Let me offer an example of how the two-way mirror works in the field of medicine.

It seems completely baffling that the human body can be healed in so many ways. If you take almost any disease like cancer, there is a typical history that the illness usually follows. Breast cancer, for example, has a known survival rate from the time of the first detected anomaly in the breast cells. Women who contract the disease will fall somewhere on the bell curve of survival. As one oncologist told me years ago, cancer is a numbers game. A statistical range will tell you at what age the disease is most likely to occur. The response of tumors to different modes of radiation and chemotherapy is constantly being documented. With these facts in hand, medicine proceeds to find a definitive cure, and if the definitive cure hasn't been found yet, science will keep working until it is.

Outside the statistical norm, however, strange things are happening. In my own medical experience, I have met the following patients:

- A young woman who told me that her mother, living on a farm in remote Vermont, developed a large tumor in her breast but decided that she was too busy to get it treated. She survived more than a decade without medical attention.

- A woman who felt a lump in her breast and decided to visualize it away. She saw hordes of white cells descending like snow to engulf the lump. After she performed this visualization for six months the lump was gone.

- A woman with a massive tumor checked out of the hospital a day before surgery because she didn't want to approach her condition out of fear and panic. She returned months later only when she felt confident of her survival. The operation succeeded and she did survive.

Every doctor has encountered the opposite side of the spectrum, women who die very quickly after receiving news of a small number of malignant cells in their breast. (In some cases, the cells are anomalous, meaning that they might be harmless, yet in a few women these anomalies quickly turn into tumors. This phenomenon was tagged long ago as "dying from the diagnosis.") I am not making recommendations about how to approach cancer, only observing that the disease often seems to reflect the beliefs brought to it by the patient. A now-famous study by David Siegel at Stanford took a group of women who had late-stage breast cancer and divided them into two groups. One group was given the best medical care, which by that point was very little. The other group sat down once a week and shared their feelings about having the disease. This alone produced a remarkable result. After two years, all the long-term survivors belonged to the second group, and the overall survival in that group was half again as long as in the group that didn't discuss their feelings. In essence, the women who confronted their emotions were able to shift the reflection in the mirror.

The human body runs on dual controls. If you heal it from the outside by material means, it will respond. If you heal it from the inside by subjective means, it will also respond. How can it be that talking about your feelings can have as much effect as a powerful cancer drug (or even more)? The answer is that consciousness always takes these two roads. It unfolds objectively as the visible universe and subjectively as events inside the mind. *Both are the same consciousness.* The same intelligence has put on two masks, differentiating into the world "out there" and the one "in here." So the wisps of feeling that arise in a cancer patient communicate with the body much like the molecules of a drug.

This phenomenon isn't remarkable anymore—all of mind-body medicine is based on the discovery of messenger molecules that begin in the brain as thoughts, beliefs, wishes, fears, and desires. The breakthrough will come when medicine stops giving all the credit to molecules. When Mozart wanted to compose a new symphony, his intention called up the necessary brain function. It would be absurd to say that Mozart's brain wanted to write a symphony first and produced messenger molecules to inform him of the fact. Awareness always comes first, and its projections, both objective and subjective, follow.

This brings us to a new principle that is crucially important, called "simultaneous interdependent co-arising." *Simultaneous* because one thing doesn't cause another. *Interdependent* because each aspect is coordinated with every other. *Co-arising* because every separate part comes from the same source.

When Mozart wanted to compose a symphony, everything associated with his creation happened simultaneously: the idea, the notes, the sound in his head, the necessary brain activity, the signals to his hands as they wrote the music down. All these ingredients were organized into one experience, and they arose together. It would be false to say that one caused the other.

If one element should fall out of place, the whole project would collapse. Should Mozart get depressed, his emotional state will block the music. Should he get physically exhausted, fatigue will block the music. One can think of a hundred ways that disorder could disrupt the picture: Mozart could have had marital problems, a stroke or heart attack, a sudden artistic block, or the noisy distraction of a two-year-old in the house.

Creation is kept from anarchy by simultaneous co-arising.

The cosmos matches the human mind far-too closely to ignore. It's as if the universe were putting on its mind-boggling show of galaxies exploding from nothingness only to tease us. It makes no sense that a process spanning billions of light years and expanding with unbelievable speed to generate trillions of stars should climax with the appearance of human DNA. Why did the universe need us to look on in wonder? Perhaps it's because reality just works that way: The unfolding cosmic drama exists simultaneously with the human brain, an instrument so finely attuned that it can delve into any level of nature. We are the ultimate audience. Nothing gets past us, no matter how minuscule or vast.

Now an extraordinary answer is beginning to dawn: *Maybe we are putting on the whole show ourselves.* The meaning of life is everything because we demand nothing less than the universe as our playground.

Quantum physics long ago conceded that the observer is the deciding factor in every observation. An electron has no fixed position in space until someone looks for it, and then the electron pops up precisely where it was looked for. Until that moment, it only exists as a wave propagating everywhere through space. That wave could collapse into a particle anywhere. Every single atom in the universe has a minute probability of being located as far away as possible or as near as possible.

The universe runs on a switch with only two positions, on and off. "On" is the material world with all its events and objects. "Off" is pure possibility, the changing room where particles go when no one is looking. The "on" position can be controlled only by external means. Once you light it up, the physical universe behaves by a set of rules. But if you catch it in the "off" position, the universe can be changed *without regard for time and space.* Nothing is heavy and immovable in the "off" position because there are no objects. Nothing is close or far away. Nothing is trapped in the past, present, or future. The "off" position is pure potential. There, your body is a set of possibilities waiting to happen, and present, too, are all those possibilities that have already happened and those that might happen. In the "off" position, everything in creation collapses down to a point, and miraculously, you live at that point; it is your source.

"On" and "off" don't give quite an accurate picture, however.

Just as there are many degrees of physical reality, there are many degrees of nonphysical reality. Your body is a solid object, a swirl of atoms, a storm of subatomic particles, and a ghost of energy, all at the same time. These states are simultaneous, but each operates according to different rules. In physics, this jumbled set of rules is called a "tangled hierarchy." The word *hierarchy* indicates that the levels are stacked in a certain order. Your body is in no danger of flying apart into random atoms because, in the hierarchy of things, solid objects stay in place, but in truth you are a cloud of electrons and a probability wave and everything in between.

That is the "on" position. In the "off" position, the same tangle continues but is totally out of sight. The invisible domain is divided in strange ways. At one level, events are all merged. Beginnings and endings meet; nothing happens without affecting everything else. But at another level, some events are more important than others; some can be controlled while others may float around with only the weakest kind of causation. By analogy, look inside your mind: Some thoughts demand to be acted on while others are passing whims; some follow strict logic while others obey very loose associations. Events in the universe are exactly the same mixed bag of potential events. If you want to, you can dive deep into the "off" position and start bringing up the events you want. You have to be prepared to meet the tangled hierarchy head on, however, because every event you might want to change is enmeshed in every other event. Still, there are certain conditions that remain the same.

DIVING INTO PURE POTENTIAL

How to Navigate the Field of Everything

1. The deeper you go, the more power is available to change things.
2. Reality flows from more subtle regions to more gross ones.

3. The easiest way to change anything is to first go to the subtlest level of it, which is awareness.
4. Still silence is the beginning of creativity. Once an event starts to vibrate, it has already begun to enter the visible world.
5. Creation proceeds by quantum leaps.
6. The beginning of an event is simultaneously its ending. The two co-arise in the domain of silent awareness.
7. Events unfold in time but are born outside of time.
8. The easiest way to create is in the evolutionary direction.
9. Since possibilities are infinite, evolution never ends.
10. The universe corresponds to the nervous system that is looking at it.

Exploring these conditions is the way you create the meaning of your own life. Let me compress these ten points into a sketch, leaving you to fill it in: The entire universe since the Big Bang behaves the way it does in order to conform to the human nervous system. If we could experience the cosmos any other way, it would be a different cosmos. The universe is lightless to a blind cave fish, which has evolved to exclude anything visual. The universe has no sound to an amoeba, no taste to a tree, no smell to a snail. Each creature selects its own range of manifestation according to its range of potential.

The universe is forced to respect your boundaries. Just as no literal vision of beauty can affect a blind cave fish and no sweetness of perfume entices a snail, any aspect of life that lies outside your boundaries will not hold meaning for you. You are like a hunter-gatherer searching the forest for food. Unless a plant is edible, you pass it by, and thus a forest full of exotic flora would be empty to you. The force of evolution is infinite, but it can work only with what the observer brings to it. A mind closed off to love, for example, will look out on a loveless world and be immune to any evidence of love, while an open mind will look out on that same world and find infinite expressions of love.

If our boundaries told the whole story, evolution could never break through them. This is where quantum leaps come in. Every observer creates a version of reality that is bound up in certain meanings and energies. As long as those meanings seem valid, the energies hold the picture together. But when the observer wants to see something new, meaning collapses, energies combine in a new way, and the world takes a quantum leap. The leap occurs on the visible plane when the switch is "on," but it was prepared in the invisible domain when the switch is "off."

Here's an example: Our ability to read came into being when pre-historic man developed a cerebral cortex, yet no one in the prehistoric world needed to read. If evolution is as random as many geneticists argue it is, the ability to read should have disappeared a million years ago, since its usefulness for survival was zero.

But this trait survived for the creature who was emerging. Consciousness knows what is to come, and it builds into every particle of creation the potential not just for one unfolding future but for *any* future. Nature doesn't have to predict what is going to happen on every level. It just opens avenues of growth, and then a given creature—in this case us—makes the leap when the time feels right. As long as potential is alive, the future can evolve by choice.

On several occasions, a sharp-eyed person spots a flaw in what I've been saying. "You're contradicting yourself. On the one hand, you claim that cause and effect go on eternally. Now you're saying that the end is already present at the beginning. Which is it?" Well, it's both. That doesn't seem like a very satisfying answer—it certainly makes sharp-eyed critics frown. But the universe is *using* cause and effect to get somewhere. When it wants to take a quantum leap, cause and effect get molded to the purpose. (Actually, you experience this every second. When you see the color red in your mind's eye, your brain cells are emitting signals in a precise way. But you didn't order them to do that; they fell into line automatically with your thought.)

236 @ Deepak Chopra

In the tangled hierarchy, an amoeba, a snail, a galaxy, a black hole, and a quark are equally valid expressions of life. Prehistoric people were as immersed in their reality as we are in ours, equally fascinated by it, and equally privileged to watch reality unfold. Evolution gives each creature exactly the world that fits its ability to perceive. But there is something above all else that needs to evolve: the gap. If you aren't ready yet to accept that the meaning of life is everything, find your own meaning in closing the gap. Fetch the world back from the brink of disaster; steer the future off a collision course with chaos. Dharma, the upholding force in Nature, will support any thought, feeling, or action that closes the gap because the universe is set up to fuse the observer and the observed.

Because you are self-aware, your fate is unity. It has been built into your brain as surely as the ability to read was built into the brain of Cro-Magnon man. As the gap closes, modern people will find themselves merging with higher and lower forms of life. All generations of humanity, from the first hominid to whatever comes after us, will be seen as one. And then what? I imagine we will take the picture off the wall, detaching ourselves from any fixed image. To live from the level of pure existence, without the need to be bound by any event in the physical world, is the end of this journey and the beginning of one never before seen. This will be the arrival of unity and the final stroke of freedom.

Changing Your Reality to Accommodate the Fourteenth Secret

The fourteenth secret is about total understanding. Understanding is not the same as thinking. Understanding is a skill developed in awareness. It's what you've made out of your potential. A baby turns into a toddler by developing the skill of walking, for example. This skill represents a quantum leap in the baby's awareness that reaches into every corner of existence: Brain patterns change; new sensations arise in the body; uncoordinated movements become coordinated; the eyes learn to view the world from an upright, forward-moving perspective; new objects in the environment come within reach; and from the threshold of the first step, the baby enters a world of unexplored possibilities that might culminate in climbing Mount Everest or running a marathon. So it's not one skill we are talking about but a true quantum leap that leaves no part of the baby's reality untouched.

The difference between a toddler and a marathon runner is that the level of understanding has deepened, not just on one front but for the whole person. Whenever you perform an action, you are actually expressing a level of understanding. In a race, two runners can be compared in such areas as mental discipline, endurance, coordination, time management, balancing obligations and relationships, and so on. When you see how far-reaching awareness really is, you begin to grasp that nothing is left out.

Understanding changes the whole picture of reality.

Being able to affect your whole reality at once is the essence of "simultaneous interdependent co-arising." There is no limit to how far your influence can reach but to find that out you must engage life with passion. When you do anything with passion, you express every aspect of who you are. Passion releases all the energy you possess. At that moment you put yourself on the line, for if you throw everything you have into a pursuit, your defects and weaknesses are also exposed. Passion brings up everything.

This inescapable fact discourages many people, who dislike the negative parts of themselves so much, or are so intimidated by them, that they hold their passion in check in the belief that life will be made safer. Perhaps it will, but at the same time they are greatly limiting their understanding of what life can bring. In general terms, there are three levels of commitment you can express:

1. Going into a situation only far enough to meet the first real obstacle
2. Going into a situation far enough to conquer some obstacles
3. Going into a situation to conquer all obstacles

Using this model, think about something you passionately wanted to do well, whether it's painting, mountaineering, writing, raising a child, or excelling in your profession. Honestly assess where you are in that endeavor.

Level 1: "I'm not satisfied with what I've accomplished. Things didn't go the way I wanted them to. Others did a lot better than I have managed to. I lost my enthusiasm and got discouraged. I still keep doing what I have to, but mostly I'm skating on the surface. I feel I have mostly failed."

Level 2: "I'm fairly satisfied with my accomplishment. I'm not always at my best but I keep up with the pack. I am counted on as someone who knows what they're doing. I've overcome a lot to get to be this good. I feel mostly like a success."

Level 3: "I mastered what I set out to do. People look up to me and consider me the old pro. I know the ins and outs of this whole thing, and I feel deep satisfaction about that. I rarely have to think anymore about what's involved. My intuition carries me along. This area of my life is a major passion."

Each level of commitment reflects the understanding you are willing to achieve. If you didn't know human nature, you might suppose that a single activity like painting, mountaineering, or writing could be treated separately, but the whole person is affected because the whole person is being expressed. (This is why it's said that you get to know yourself on the mountain or in front of the blank canvas.) Even if you pick a very narrow skill, like running a marathon or cooking, your whole sense of self shifts when you succeed with passion as opposed to failing or backing off.

The willingness to reach inside every part of yourself opens the door to total understanding. You place your entire identity on the line, not just an isolated part. This may sound daunting, but actually it's the most natural way to approach any situation. When you hold some part of yourself in reserve you deny it exposure to life; you repress its energy and keep it from understanding what it needs to know. Imagine a baby who wants to walk but has these reservations:

1. I don't want to look bad.
2. I don't want to fall down.
3. I don't want anyone else to watch me fail.
4. I don't want to live with the burden of failure.
5. I don't want to expend all my energy.
6. I don't want any pain.
7. I want to get things over with as fast as possible.

For a baby these reservations seem absurd. If any of them applied, learning to walk would never happen, or it would happen tentatively. The chance for mastery could never present itself. Yet as adults we resort to these reservations all the time. We deny ourselves mastery as a result. No one can change the fact that all the negatives of a situation express themselves the minute the situation arises, along with all the positives. There is no escaping the internal decisions we've made.

Everything you've decided about yourself is in play at this moment.

Fortunately, these individual decisions can be reexamined and changed. Since all the negatives are right in front of you, you don't have to go searching for them. What people experience as obstacles in life are reflections of a decision to shut out understanding. If you shut out too much understanding, you become a victim, subject to forces that bewilder and overwhelm you. These forces aren't blind fate or misfortune; they are holes in your awareness, the places where you haven't been able to look.

Today, try to look at one of the decisions that has kept you from totally engaging in life, which may be included in the list just above.

I don't want to look bad: This decision involves self-image. "Looking good" means preserving an image, but images are just frozen pictures. They give the most superficial impression of who you are. Most people find it too hard to get past self-image. They fashion a certain look, a certain way of acting, a certain level of style, taste, lifestyle, and status that gets assembled into who they think they are. Their self-image is applied to every new situation with only one possible outcome: They look either good or bad. Long ago such people decided that they would never look bad if they could help it.

This decision can be countered only by your willingness to forget how you look. I'm sure you've seen slow-motion films of Olympic runners crossing the finish line, drenched in sweat, their faces distorted with effort, expending every last ounce of themselves. In their passion to win they haven't the slightest care about how they look. This gives a clue to your own situation: If you are really focused on the process at hand, you won't consider your appearance.

Today, take the following ideas and follow them through until you understand how they apply to you:

- Winning doesn't have to look good. The two have nothing to do with each other.
- Being passionate about something looks good from the inside, which is where it really counts.
- Looking good from the inside isn't an image. It's a feeling of satisfaction.
- You won't be satisfied as long as image is on your mind.

I don't want to fall down: This decision revolves around failure, which in turn revolves around judgment. In the field of painting, every masterpiece is preceded by a sketch. Sometimes these sketches amount to a few rough scribbles; sometimes they require years and dozens of tries. Did the painter fail when he made a sketch? No, because it takes stages of development to master a skill. If you judge your early efforts to be failures, you are putting yourself at odds with a natural process.

People who are afraid to fall down usually were ridiculed or humiliated in the past. This is one area where parents pass on negative judgments with terrible effect—failing is something you inherit from someone who discouraged you. Fear gets attached to failure by connecting it to sense of self. "Falling down means I'm worthless." Next to looking bad, the second most crippling mental reservation is fear of falling down and feeling like a worthless person.

Today, face yourself honestly and confront how much of this fear is inside you. The degree to which you judge yourself is the degree to which you need to heal. Most people say they hate to fail, but behind the word *hate* can be a wide range of emotions, from devastating collapse of the self to mild annoyance at not doing your best. You can sense where you belong on the scale. Give yourself a rating:

- I feel devastated when I fail. I can't shake the feeling for days, and when I look back at my biggest failings I relive how intense the humiliation was.

- I feel bad enough when I fail that I usually walk away. It takes a lot for me to get back on the horse, but eventually I will. It's a matter of pride and self-respect.

- I take failure in stride because it's more important to accomplish what I want to do. I learn from my failures. There's something positive in every setback. If you can learn from your mistakes you haven't failed.

- I don't think in terms of winning and losing. I stay centered and watch how I perform in any situation. Each response shows me a new aspect of myself. I want to understand everything, and from that perspective each experience is like turning a new page in the book of evolution.

Having assessed where you stand, develop a program for change that is suitable to that stage.

First, people at this level are oversensitive to setbacks and take them so personally that they keep reopening old wounds. If this is you, go back to the basics. Find something very minor to accomplish, such as making an omelet or jogging around the block. Set aside time to do this activity, and as you are engaged in it, feel what it's like to succeed. Be like a good parent and praise yourself. If things go a bit wrong, tell yourself that it's all right. You need to reformat how you feel about setting a goal and reaching it.

Inside you there is a discouraging voice that you notice too quickly and give too much credence to. Slowly develop a connection to the voice of encouragement. That is also inside you but has been drowned out by the voice of criticism. Gradually increase the challenges you are able to face. Go from making an omelet for yourself to making one for someone else. Feel what it's like to be praised. Absorb the fact that you deserve this praise. Don't compare yourself to anyone else—you are where you are and nowhere else. Keep reinforcing your successes.

At least once every day, do something that looks like a success in your eyes and that earns you praise from either yourself or someone else. Be sure that the external praise is sincere. It will take time, but you will notice after a while that the voice of encouragement inside you is beginning to grow. You will learn to rely on it, and you will come to understand that it is right about you.

Second, people at this level feel bad enough about falling down that they often walk away from new challenges, yet they don't feel so

bad that they are devastated. If this is you, you need more motivation because you are on the cusp of wanting to win but are reluctant
to risk failure. You could tip one way or the other. To increase your
motivation, you can join a team or find a coach. Team spirit will help
you override the discouraging voices inside you. A coach will keep
you focused so that walking away is not an option. Pick a level of
activity that won't overtax your self-confidence. It's more important
to internalize the elements of success than to conquer a big challenge.
A team doesn't have to mean sports—find any group that has esprit
de corps. It could be a jazz band, a volunteer group, or a political
party. External support will help you over your internal hurdles. You
will come to understand that those hurdles aren't mountains; they
can be whittled down into small peaks of achievement.

Third, people at this level are more encouraged by success than
discouraged by failure. They have positive motivation in good sup-
ply. If this is you, you may succeed for a long time but eventually
find that external rewards are no longer satisfying. You need to set a
completely internal goal for yourself in order to grow. Among the
most valuable internal goals are learning to be more intimate, learning to serve others without reward, and learning about the depths of
spirituality. Aim to gain more understanding of yourself without any
outside accomplishment. Over time, the distinction between success
and failure will begin to soften. You will start to see that everything
you've ever done has been about the unfolding of yourself to yourself.
The greatest satisfactions in life come about when that unfolding is
the only thing you need.

Fourth, people at this level have conquered failure. They enjoy
every twist and turn in life, being satisfied with experience of every
kind. If this is you, aim to deepen your mastery. Your remaining
obstacles are subtle and belong at the level of ego. You still believe
that an isolated self is having these experiences. Aim for detachment
and expansion beyond this limited self. For you, the deepest spiritual

texts and a personal commitment to one of the four paths will bring great satisfaction.

I don't want anyone else to watch me fail: This decision revolves around shame. Shame is the internalized fear of the opinion of others. Their disapproval becomes your shame. The cliché that people from the East cannot bear to "lose face" refers to shame, which can be a powerful social force. The answer to shame isn't to become shameless in your behavior. Many people try that solution as teenagers, hoping that their intense self-consciousness can be overcome by external acts of bravado, like joyriding or dressing outlandishly. If you easily feel ashamed, you've made an internal decision that needs to be changed.

First, realize that what others think about you is often dependent on whether your actions are good or bad in *their* eyes. Social judgment is inescapable, and we are all affected by it. However, others will try to shame you through words, tone of voice, and behavior. Stand aside from your own situation and watch how this works. Read a tabloid or watch a celebrity gossip show. Be aware of the constant stream of insinuation and judgment. Get comfortable with the fact that such treatment of others exists. You aren't here to change it, only to become aware of how it works.

Second, withdraw from shaming others. This behavior is a disguise for you. You think that if you gossip, tear people down, try to look superior, or in any other way go on the attack, you will find protection from your own vulnerability. In reality, all you are doing is immersing yourself in the culture of shame. Step away; you can't afford to be there any longer.

Third, find ways to earn praise that makes you feel like a good person. This is different from praise for what you accomplish. You no doubt can do many things that would get somebody else to say you did a good job. But what you lack is praise that heals your sense of shame. That can come only when emotions are at stake. You need to feel the warmth of someone else's gratitude; you need to see admiration for you in somebody's eyes. I'd suggest service to the poor, the elderly, or the sick. Devote some time in a volunteer program to help the needy in any way that you define that term. Until you reconnect on the basis of love, with no hint of personal criticism, you won't be able to separate yourself from feelings of shame.

I don't want to live with the burden of failure: This decision revolves around guilt. Guilt is the internal knowledge of wrongdoing. As such, it has its place as a healthy reminder from your conscience. But when guilt gets attached to the wrong thing, it can be destructive and unhealthy. Guilty people suffer most from the inability to tell thoughts from deeds. They are burdened by things that are purely mental rather than actions in the world. Sometimes this is called "sinning in your heart." Whatever name you give to it, guilt makes you feel like a failure because of your horrible past.

Guilty people don't want to face new challenges for fear that when they fail, they will feel more guilty, adding to the burden of the past. To them this sounds reasonable, but in actuality, guilt itself is extremely unreasonable. As with shame, you can break guilt down into its irrational components:

- Guilt doesn't accurately measure good and bad. It can make you suffer for trivial reasons.

- Guilt is a blanket that tries to cover everything. It makes you feel guilty about people and things that have no bearing on your guilty actions except that they happen to be in the vicinity.

- Guilt makes you feel overly responsible. You believe you caused bad things to happen that in truth had nothing to do with you.

• Guilt is prejudiced. It finds you wrong all the time without any chance of reprieve.

When you understand these four things you can begin to apply them to yourself. Don't try to force guilt to go away. Have your guilty reaction, let it be what it is, but then ask yourself: "Did I really do something bad?" "Would I condemn someone else who did the same thing?" "Did I do the best I could under the circumstances?" These questions help you get a more objective sense of good and bad. If you find yourself in doubt, seek the opinion of a nonguilty, noncondemning person.

"Who did I actually hurt?" Be specific; don't let guilt be a blanket. You may find that you've never really hurt anyone. If you still think you have, go to the person and ask how he or she feels. Discuss your actions. Try to reach the point where you can ask forgiveness. When it is given, accept it as genuine. Write the forgiveness down as a mental note. Whenever your guilty voice accuses you again, hold up the piece of paper that proves you've been forgiven, saying, "See? It doesn't matter how you try and make me feel. The person I actually harmed doesn't care anymore."

"Am I really responsible here? What part did I really play? Were my actions a small part of the situation or a big part?" You can be responsible only for the actions you took or failed to take. Be specific. Detail those actions to yourself; don't exaggerate them and don't fall for the irrational notion that just by being there you are totally responsible. Many family situations immerse us in a general sense of shared guilt, but if you are specific and narrow your responsibility to what you actually said and did, not what others around you said and did, you can diffuse the guilt trip of being responsible for everything.

"What good things have I done to atone for the bad ones? When will I have done enough to let go? Am I ready to forgive myself?" All bad actions have their limit, after which you are forgiven and reprieved from guilt. But as we've seen, the inner voice of guilt is prejudiced—you are guilty the moment you step into the courtroom and will remain so forever. Take any guilty action and write down the day you will be forgiven. Do everything you can to atone for your bad action, and when the day of release arrives, take your pardon and walk away. No heinous action deserves condemnation forever; don't buy into the prejudice that would hold you responsible for even your most venial sins year after year.

I don't want to expend all my energy: This decision revolves around a belief that energy, like the money in your bank account, is limited. Some people who don't want to spend much energy avoid new challenges out of laziness, but that is mostly a disguise for deeper issues. It's certainly true that energy is limited, but if you have ever committed yourself passionately to anything, you've found that the more energy you devote to it, the more you have. Passion replenishes itself.

What drains energy, strangely enough, is the act of holding back. The more you conserve your energy, the more narrow become the channels through which it can flow. People who are afraid to love, for example, wind up constricting love's expression. They feel tight in the heart rather than expanded; loving words stick in their throats; they find it awkward to make even small loving gestures. Tightness develops fear of expansion, and thus the snake keeps eating its own tail: The less energy you spend, the less you have to spend. Here are a few steps that can cause the channels of energy to expand:

- Learn to give. When you feel most like hoarding, turn to someone in need and offer some of what you possess in abundance. This doesn't have to be money or goods. You can give time and attention, which actually will do much more to open your channels of energy than giving away cash.

• Be generous. This means generous in praise and appreciation even more than generous with your money. Most people hunger for praise and get much less than they deserve. Be the first to notice when someone has done well. Appreciate from a full heart and not just with formulaic words. Praise in detail, showing the other person that you actually paid attention to what he or she accomplished. Meet the person with your gaze and stay connected as you praise.

• Follow your passion. Some area in your life makes you want to spend all your energy there. For most people, there's a built-in inhibition about going too far, however, so they don't really spend themselves even in those areas. Be willing to go the limit, and then go a bit further. If you like to hike, set your sights on a mountain and conquer it. If you like to write, start and finish a book. The point is not to force yourself but to prove how much energy is really there. Energy is the carrier of awareness; it allows awareness to come out into the world. By devoting more energy to any endeavor you increase the reward of understanding that will come to you.

I don't want any pain: This decision revolves around several issues, all having to do with psychological rather than physical pain. The first issue is suffering in the past. People who have suffered without being able to find healing have a great aversion to any new possibility of pain. Another issue is weakness. If pain has defeated someone in the past, the prospect of more pain brings up fear of getting even weaker. Finally, there is the issue of vulnerability. Pain makes us feel exposed and more prone to further pain than if we remained invulnerable. All these issues run deep, and it's rare to find anyone who is immune to them. As always, there are degrees of sensitivity here.

Pain is neutral in the cosmic design. In the material world, pain motivates us negatively while pleasure motivates us positively. Learning to be free means that your actions don't depend on throwing either switch. No challenge is greater, given that all of us are deeply attached to the cycle of pleasure and pain. Only by reaching the state of witnessing can you observe how uncomfortable you feel when either pleasure or pain drives you onward.

I want to get things over with as fast as possible: This decision revolves around impatience. When your mind is restless and disorganized, you can't help but be impatient. You lack the attention span needed for taking time and being patient. People who hold back because they can't pay enough attention are also deprived of new challenges. Their understanding is forced to remain on a very superficial level. Ironically, time is not essential to a thoughtful response. It's not how long you pay attention but how deep that counts.

In the movie *Amadeus,* a very proficient composer, Salieri, was tormented by the genius of his rival, Mozart. Mozart wasn't a better person than Salieri—for the movie's sake Mozart was turned into a vain, childish hedonist. He didn't spend more time composing than Salieri; he didn't have greater favor from patrons; he didn't go to music school longer. Salieri blamed God for this gross inequality in gifts, and unconsciously most of us do the same when we confront somebody who vastly exceeds our abilities.

Impatience is rooted in frustration. We refuse to pay attention because the results aren't coming fast enough or with enough rewards. The mind prefers to hop away from this potential source of discomfort. If you find that you're easily made impatient, you probably blame outside circumstances. Traffic isn't moving fast enough; the grocery checkout line takes forever; when you ask someone to do a job the person always drags his feet.

Projecting your impatience on the outside world is a defense, a way of deflecting a fear of inadequacy. In the most extreme cases of attention deficit disorder, particularly among young children, this fear always underlies the surface inattention. Impatient people are too discouraged to go inside very deeply. Even without a rival of Mozart's commanding genius, all of us are intimidated by a shadowy competitor inside—someone who by definition is better than we are. This ghost drives us out of our own awareness.

Impatience ends when you can go back inside yourself with enough confidence to let awareness unfold. Confidence cannot be forced. You will be adequate in your own eyes when you experience deeper and deeper levels of understanding. If you are impatient, you need to face the reality that you aren't the best at everything, nor do you need to be. Stop yourself when you feel overshadowed by greater genius, talent, wealth, status, or accomplishment. The only real person inside you is you. That person is a seed whose growth is unlimited. The way you make seeds grow is with nourishment, and in this case that nourishment comes from paying attention. Be willing to face yourself, whatever you think your shortcomings are. Only a direct encounter with yourself brings the nourishment of attention, and the more nourishment you offer, the greater your growth will be.

❀

EVERYTHING IS PURE ESSENCE

AT LAST, EVERY LAYER OF THE ONION has been peeled away. We come face to face with the indescribable, the secret at the core of life. Yet words have almost reached their limit.

What do you have when you find yourself facing the indescribable? You can only try with inadequate words to describe it. The mind can't help itself. Used to putting everything into a thought, it cannot grasp *something* beyond thought.

We each draw a world of line, form, and color using invisible ink. Our instrument is no more than a speck of consciousness, like a pencil point moving across a blank piece of paper. Yet everything pours out of that single point. Could anything be more mysterious and at the same time more miraculous? A point infinitely smaller than a pencil point draws the shape of the universe.

That point is made of essence, or the purest form of Being. Essence is the ultimate mystery because it manages to do three things at once:

It conceives everything in existence.
It turns what it has imagined into reality.
It enters that reality and keeps it alive.

Right now you are also performing these three activities. Before anything happens to you it is conceived in the imagination—that is, in the state where wisps of images and desires are born. These images then unfold into expressed objects and events. While that happens you enter the event subjectively, which means you absorb it into your nervous system. The simplest way to describe this three-part act of creation is to say that you imagine a picture, then you paint it and finally step inside.

All that is required to find the essence of life is to step outside the picture and see yourself. You won't see a person or even a soul, just a speck of awareness—the point that is producing the most lovely, appalling, mundane, holy, astonishing, ordinary, and marvelous pictures. But even in using these words, I have fallen into the temptation of trying to describe the indescribable. Let me throw every image away and say the simplest things that are true: I exist, I am aware, I create. These are the three qualities of essence that permeate the universe.

With every unreal aspect of yourself stripped away, only essence remains. Once you realize that essence is the real you, the golden door opens. Essence is precious because it is the stuff from which the soul is made. If you could keep holding on to essence while stepping back into the picture you create, you would be living from the level of the soul at every moment.

But a huge difficulty arises that keeps the golden door shut: Nothing *isn't* essence. When you reduce the one reality to its essence, every quality disappears. Now a tree, a horse, a cloud, and a human being are the same. Physical dimensions also disappear. The time elapsed between any two events is now zero; the space between any two objects is zero. Light and dark no longer exist. Complete fullness and utter emptiness are the same.

In other words, at the very moment you think you have the secret to everything, you look down to find that your hands are empty. This is a particularly disturbing outcome for those who travel the spiritual path to find God. Unless you define God as essence, he will vanish also. But in India, there is a strong tradition that puts essence far above a personal god. One of the greatest modern spiritual teachers, Nisargadatta Maharaj, made no concessions on this point. He declared himself—and all other people—to be pure essence. As a result, he met with a good deal of contentious opposition.

Here's a typical interchange from a skeptical visitor to Maharaj:

Q: Did God create the earth for you?
A: God is my devotee and did all this for me.
Q: Is there no god apart from you?
A: How can there be? "I am" is the root, God is the tree. Whom am I to worship, and what for?
Q: Are you the devotee or the object of devotion?
A: Neither. I am devotion itself.

You can feel the baffled frustration in the questioner's voice, and who can blame him? The path to unity is so different from what is taught in organized religion that it bends the mind. Maharaj used to regularly announce that we were not created for God, God was created for us. By which he meant that essence, being invisible, had to create an almighty projection to be worshipped. By itself, essence has no qualities; there is nothing to hold on to.

Essence does a vanishing act because it's not anything you can feel or think about. Since being alive consists of feeling and thinking, how is essence going to be of any use? At the most superficial level, essence is not useful because differences still hold your attention. Let's say that you want to be happy rather than unhappy, rich rather than poor, good rather than evil. None of these distinctions matters to your essence. Essence works with only three things: It exists, it creates, it is aware.

A life without differences sounds completely unlivable, and yet there is a document that talks about essence in a matter-of-fact way, suggesting that somebody has figured out how to live from this level. The document, known as the *Yoga Vashistha,* has many strange things to offer. *Yoga* we know means "unity," and *Vashistha* is the name of the author; therefore, in Sanskrit the title means "Vashistha's version of unity." No one has offered proof that a person by this name ever lived—the text itself is many centuries old—but Vashistha's version of unity stands as a unique work. I believe it is the furthest stretch the human nervous system has ever taken toward being aware of existence itself.

Some typical observations by Vashistha quickly give you the flavor of his viewpoint on life:

> In the infinite consciousness universes come and go like particles
> of dust in a beam of sunlight that shines through a hole in
> the roof.
> Death is ever keeping a watch over our life.
> All objects are experienced in the subject and nowhere else.
> Whole worlds arise and fall like ripples in the ocean.

Vashistha's teaching has a reputation for being one of the most difficult, abstract texts in the spiritual canon, and therefore not for beginners. I read him much more simply as the voice of essence. Even from a handful of sayings, some general themes emerge clearly. Vashistha considers the universe to be impermanent and fleeting. He observes that death is inescapably linked to life. He uses subjective awareness as the true measure of what's real, compared to which the material world is like a puff of air.

As you keep reading, these themes get elaborated hundreds of times over with such total conviction that the reader becomes mesmerized. The sentences sound arcane, sometimes inconceivable, but then that is the point—this is life compressed into ideas as dense as diamonds:

> Whatever the mind thinks of, that alone it sees.
> What people call fate or divine will is nothing other than action from the past acting upon itself.
> Even as motion is inherent in air, manifestation is inherent in consciousness.

As you pore over his words, it's easy to fall into a kind of trance in which the visible world blows away like a feather. The effect isn't to inspire or uplift: Vashistha offers absolutely no consolation. Nothing matters to him except essence, and therefore he is the ultimate teacher on the subject of getting real. Getting real is the goal of this book, too, and therefore I've tried to distill Vashistha's advice on how to live if you are totally serious about waking up from unreality. He describes four conditions that must exist if you want to find reality:

Contentment
Inquiry
Self-awareness
Strength

Four ordinary, somewhat innocuous words. What did he mean by them, this sage who knew essence perhaps better than anyone who ever lived?

Contentment: This is the quality of restfulness in the mind. Someone who is content exists without doubt and fear. Doubt is a constant reminder that there is no answer to the mystery of life, or that all answers will turn out to be untrustworthy. Fear is a constant reminder that you can be hurt. As long as either of these beliefs exists in your mind, resting easy in yourself is impossible. So contentment must be won on the level where doubt and fear have been defeated.

Inquiry: To get real, you have to question the unreal over and over until it disappears. This process is a kind of peeling away. You look at something that seems reliable and trustworthy, and if it betrays your trust, you say, "No, this isn't it," and throw it away. The next thing that asks for your trust also gets examined, and if it proves unreliable, you peel it away as well. Layer by layer, you keep inquiring until you reach something that is completely trustworthy, and that thing must be real.

Self-Awareness: This quality tells you where to conduct your inquiry—not outside in the material world, but in yourself. Turning inward doesn't happen as a single step. For every challenge there are always two solutions—inner and outer. Only by working through every reason to look outward are you left with why you should look inward.

Strength: Because you are looking inward, no one from the outside can help you. This implies a kind of isolation and solitude that only the strong can accept. Strength is not a given; it's not that the strong are born different from the weak. Your inner strength grows from experience. The first stages of looking inward give you a hint that you can get real, and with that bit of added strength you move forward. You grow in resolve and certainty. You test what you find out until it feels secure. Step by step you discover that strength is built from experience. The journey itself makes you strong.

Vashistha has almost nothing else to say about everyday matters. No one has to start living a certain way or stop living a certain way in order to get real. Vashistha's viewpoint is totally accepting: He is content to allow life to unfold. "For only as long as one invests any object with reality," he says, "that bondage lasts; once that notion goes, with it goes bondage." In other words, unreality has to melt away on its own. Until it does, you can be rich or poor, happy or sad, certain or plagued with doubt, as your karma dictates.

Vashistha feels infinite tolerance because "the unreal has no existence and the real will never stop existing." He feels infinitely serene
because "consciousness is omnipresent, pure, tranquil, omnipotent."
Yet it's not for these deep thoughts that I hold Vashistha to be
unique. His special gift lies in jabs of truth that are as sharp as salt
on the tongue: "The universe is one long dream. The ego-sense, along
with the fancy that there are other people, is as unreal as anything in
a dream."

When I see Vashistha in my mind's eye, I envision a picnic where
everyone has fallen asleep under the shade of an old spreading beech
tree, done in by too much food and pleasure and play. Only one person is sitting up, awake and alert, waiting for the others to end their
nap. *Everyone else is asleep.* There is no escaping that jab of truth.
Vashistha knows he is alone, but he isn't a pessimist. His solitary
watch hasn't calloused over his love for other people. Essence *is* love.
Not the love of passing emotion or the love that gets attached to one
person but the sheer love of being here. By comparison, the emotional kind of love is confined, doubtful, full of fear, and driven by
dreams that never get fully realized.

In pure essence, Vashistha knew that he had found the secret of
universal happiness. That secret has three parts: freedom from all
limitation, complete knowledge of creation, and immortality.
Vashistha found all three. That such a condition is possible proves
the existence of love, since nothing more could be wished for. Until
the moment when these three things are achieved, every other awakening is false; the whole universe exists in the dream state, the pursuit of a cosmic delusion.

This delusion has now been presented to you in full. It consists
of separation, fragmentation, the loss of wholeness. There must be
a final "No!" that refuses to participate in the delusion, and
Vashistha has said it, loud and clear. He is often the one teacher I
reach for when I imagine that I am in trouble. Reading his words,
I can feel myself rising to his level, not fully and not permanently,

but with enough validity that I come away feeling reassured. There are times when I want CNN to stop running endless crises in the crawl space at the bottom of the television screen and start running these words instead so that people can be reminded about what's real:

> Whatever is in the mind is like a city in the clouds.
> The emergence of this world is no more than thoughts coming into manifestation.
> From the infinite consciousness we have created each other in our imagination.
> As long as there is "you" and an "I," there is no liberation. Dear ones, we are all cosmic consciousness assuming individual form.

It's nearly impossible perhaps to take these noble sentiments into the rough and tumble of everyday life, but the basic thing that Vashistha wants us to do is to live from essence—and that *is* workable. The teacher I mentioned before, Nisargadatta Maharaj, lived such a life. As a young man he was raised on a farm to walk behind a pair of oxen pulling a plow. But spirituality intrigued him and he made his way to a guru who gave him one piece of advice: "You are the unborn and undying 'I am.' Remember that, and if your mind wanders from this truth, bring it back." The young Maharaj went away, needing no more visits to gurus, and found his essence with that simple teaching.

The most exalted state of awareness comes down to realizing how commonplace it actually is to live a cosmic life. We do it all the time. One only has to listen to how matter-of-factly Vashistha looks around and sees infinity in every direction. His is the teaching to keep by your bed when you want to do something other than fall asleep:

To a suffering person, a night is an epoch. To a reveler, a night passes like a moment. In a dream, a moment is no different from an epoch. But to the sage, whose consciousness has overcome all limitations, there is no day or night. As one turns away from the notion of "I" and "the world," one finds liberation.

CHANGING YOUR REALITY TO ACCOMMODATE THE FIFTEENTH SECRET

The fifteenth lesson is about unity. As a young man, I was driven to reach as far as I could, but over time I began to grasp that unity is not an achievement one can set for oneself in the way one can set winning a game or finding the perfect wife or rising to the top of a profession. Unity is more like music. Bach might visit a kindergarten class and inspire the children with hope that they can all be like him. In reality, few children will ever grow up with Bach's genius for music. But they don't have to. Music is a glorious pursuit on its own, comparing yourself to no one. Every moment of music making brings delight on its own, not just as a step up the mountain toward the highest peak.

Spirituality can bring delight at every moment—or at least every day—if it is pursued with the four things in mind that Vashistha taught. Let's review them again, this time as they might be applied to our own lives.

Contentment: Look for a moment of contentment every day. You have a right to it because, in the cosmic design, you are safe and cared for. Be content not with your lot in life but with being here in the flow of life. The glories of creation are in your very cells; you are made of the same mindstuff as the angels, the stars, and God himself.

Inquiry: Don't let a day go by without asking who you are. Understanding is a skill, and like all skills it must be coaxed into existence. To understand who you are means returning again and again to the question, Who am I? Each time you return you are allowing a new ingredient to enter your awareness. Every day is filled with the potential for expanding your awareness, and although each new addition may seem tiny, overall the accumulation will be great. It may take thousands of days to know who you are; it takes only one day to quit asking. Don't let today be that day.

Self-awareness: Never forget that you are not in the world; the world is in you. Whatever you need to know about existence will arise nowhere outside yourself. When anything happens to you, take the experience inward. Creation is set up to bring you constant hints and clues about your role as a co-creator. Be aware of them; absorb them. Your soul is metabolizing experience as surely as your body is metabolizing food.

Strength: No one will ever be able to say that walking the spiritual path is the easiest thing in the world—or the hardest. The birth of the new is too intimately tied to the death of the old. Joy comes on the heels of sorrow, as it must if birth and death are merged. Don't expect one or the other today. Use your strength to meet whatever is coming your way. Be as committed and passionate about spirituality as you can be. Strength is the foundation for passion, and you were designed to survive and thrive no matter how life unfolds. Be strong today in that knowledge.

❁

SECOND BIRTH

AT A CERTAIN POINT life has no more secrets to reveal. You live as if there is one reality, and in return it repays you richly. The fear born of duality is gone, replaced by an unshakable contentment. Awareness has become fully aware of itself. When we reach this stage of freedom, life starts over, which is why enlightenment is rightly called a second birth.

Growing up in India, I never met an enlightened person. My family was deeply religious, particularly on my mother's side. But when I was born the whole country was caught up in the turmoil of a political birth, as the English decamped overnight and left us to suffer our birth pangs alone. These were terrible times: Rioting and wholesale killing raged unchecked, as religious intolerance led to violence throughout North India.

When Mahatma Gandhi was assassinated by a religious fanatic on January 30, 1948, the killer claimed another victim. A thread. The traditional costume of the Brahmin caste included a double thread worn over the shoulder. There were many evils in the caste system, but in my mind the double thread symbolized a deep truth—that enlightenment was possible. Until modern times, every-one in India knew that the double thread was the promise of a sec-ond birth. It stood for a legacy going back before memory began. Today, enlightenment is no longer the goal of life, not even in India. The most that any teacher can do is to open the door again; he can answer three questions in the age-old way:

- *Who am I?* You are the totality of the universe acting through a human nervous system.
- *Where did I come from?* You came from a source that was never born and will never die.
- *Why am I here?* To create the world in every moment.

To gain this knowledge for oneself is like being pushed through the birth canal again. You may utter a cry of surprise—and perhaps of shock and pain—at finding yourself in an unknown world. Once you accept this second birth, you continue to have thoughts and feel-ings, but now they are soft impulses against a background of silent awareness, faint ripples that rise and fall without disturbing the ocean of being.

I can't help feeling that enlightenment was never India's prize to possess—or any culture's. The second birth comes from looking at life as it already is, seeing it from the still point inside. To the degree that anyone does that, they are enlightened. The universe goes to the still point in order to create time and space. You go there to fetch a word or the memory of a face or the scent of a rose. At this very moment, the world is blossoming into its infinite variety before falling silent in amazement at the miracle it has just achieved.

Index

ABOUT THE AUTHOR

DEEPAK CHOPRA is the author of more than fifty books translated in over thirty-five languages, including numerous *New York Times* bestsellers in both the fiction and non fiction categories. Chopra's Wellness Radio airs weekly on Sirius Stars, Channel 102 which focuses on the areas of success, love, sexuality and relationships, well being, and spirituality. He is founder and president of the Alliance for a New Humanity and can be contacted at www.deepakchopra.com. *Time* magazine heralds Deepak Chopra as one of the top 100 heroes and icons of the century, and credits him as "the poet-prophet of alternative medicine."

www.deepakchopra.com

Also by

DEEPAK
CHOPRA

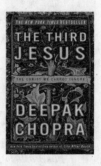

*The Ultimate
Happiness Prescription*
7 Keys to Joy and Enlightenment
$19.99 hardcover
(Canada: $24.99)
978-0-307-58971-2

*Reinventing the Body,
Resurrecting the Soul*
How to Create a New You
$15.00 paper
(Canada: $17.00)
978-0-307-45298-6

The Third Jesus
The Christ We Cannot Ignore
$15.00 paper
(Canada: $18.95)
978-0-307-33832-7

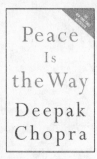

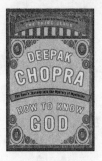

Peace Is the Way
Bringing War and Violence
to an End
$16.00 paper
(Canada: $19.00)
978-0-307-33981-2

Grow Younger,
Live Longer
Ten Steps to Reverse Aging
$14.95 paper
(Canada: $21.00)
978-0-609-81008-8

How to Know God
The Soul's Journey into the
Mystery of Mysteries
$16.00 paper
(Canada: $19.00)
978-0-609-80523-7

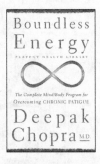

The Path to Love
Spiritual Strategies
for Healing
$15.00 paper
(Canada: $17.00)
978-0-609-80135-2

Boundless Energy
The Complete Mind/Body
Program for Overcoming
Chronic Fatigue
$13.95 paper
(Canada: $17.95)
978-0-609-80075-1

AVAILABLE WHEREVER BOOKS ARE SOLD